GIRLS' VOICES

Girls' Voices

supporting girls' learning and emotional development

Leora Cruddas
and
Lynda Haddock

Trentham Books
Stoke on Trent, UK and Sterling USA

Trentham Books Limited

Westview House	22883 Quicksilver Drive
734 London Road	Sterling
Oakhill	VA 20166-2012
Stoke on Trent	USA
Staffordshire	
England ST4 5NP	

2003 © Trentham Books

First published 2003

British Library Cataloguing-in-Publication Data
A catalogue record for this book is available from the British Library

ISBN 1 85856 277 5

Typeset by Gabrielle, Chester
Printed in Great Britain by Cromwell Press Ltd., Wiltshire.

Contents

Acknowledgements

Many girls and teachers gave their time to this project. They generously shared their thoughts and feelings as they reflected together on their experiences of school. We want to record our warmest thanks to all of them.

A number of voluntary organisations contributed to the project. Their ideas and energy were invaluable and we want to thank them too. We would particularly like to thank those organisations who contributed to the Girls' Symposium at the East Ham Town Hall, and Yasmin Raza for almost single-handedly organising this very successful day.

Professor Valerie Hey gave important and useful guidance and support throughout the project. We were all inspired by her enthusiasm, commitment and advice.

Special thanks to Jo Robinson for her invaluable training in the techniques of developmental group work.

Finally, thanks go to the DfES who funded this research.

The project team members were:
Patsy Burke, Sue Dawn, Yasmin Raza, Sue East, Marie Healy, Marilyn Martin, Jenny McBarnette, Glen Pierre, Jackie Smith, Debbie Crossman, Tina Vallely, Lynda Haddock and Leora Cruddas.

This book was written by Leora Cruddas and Lynda Haddock in the spirit of collaboration, using written accounts of the work in school and interview transcriptions prepared by the project team members. We are particularly grateful to Sue Dawn and Jackie Smith for their analysis of the material in chapters 6 and 7.

Abbreviations

CAT	Cognitive Ability Tests
CSIE	Centre for Studies for Inclusive Education
DfEE:	Department for Education and Employment
DfES	Department for Education and Skills
EAL	English as an Additional Language
EBD	Emotional and Behavioural Difficulties
EiC	Excellence in Cities
ESRC	Economic and Social Research Council
GCSE	General Certificate of Secondary Education
ICT	Information and Communication Technology
IT	Information Technology
KS3	Key Stage 3
KS4	Key Stage 4
LEA	Local Education Authority
LSU	Learning Support Unit
NACCCE	National Advisory Committee on Creative and Cultural Education
NAWP	Newham Asian Women's Project
NQT	Newly Qualified Teacher
PE	Physical Education
PMT	Pre-menstrual tension
PSHE	Personal, Social and Health Education
PSE	Personal and Social Education
QCA	Qualification and Curriculum Authority
RE	Religious Education
SATs	Standardised Assessment Tests
SEN	Special Educational Needs
SENCO	Special Educational Needs Co-ordinator
TTA	Teacher Training Agency
TES	*The Times Educational Supplement*
YAP	Youth Awareness Programme

Preface

This is not a book like any other: it is a work in progress, and that progress depends on you. (Boal, 1998 pix)

At the beginning of his book on legislative theatre, Boal gives a set of instructions about how to use the book, permission (as it were) not to read the whole book from cover to cover. He suggests that readers find their own path through the material and provides some clues for how to do that.

Similarly, we would like to offer you a series of clues for finding your own way through this work in progress.

If you want to know what we were thinking about and what policy developments were happening during our project, read **Rights and wrongs – developments in the policy field**. This section is fairly theoretical and looks at some big political questions.

If you want to know about the methods that informed our thinking, read **How we made it work**; but if you want to know how we organised groups and worked with the young women, read **Setting up developmental group work**. The methodology section is the theory behind the practice of using developmental group work. **Practical accounts of school based project work** that contain useful descriptions of pioneering and original interventions can be found in chapter 5. We hope that these case studies of good practice will inspire other professionals to attempt similar interventions in schools.

We think that the most important section in this book is what the young women with whom we worked thought about barriers to learning (chapter 6), what support they needed to learn and become emotionally healthy people (chapter 7) and what they thought about the project, the methods we were using and whether they saw benefit in the group work (chapter 8). In chapter 8, Space to talk: how the girls saw the benefits of group work, we critically consider some of the girls' responses and begin to reflect on the methods we used in our efforts to create a more inclusive and participatory process in our research. This chapter begins to explore the benefits of group work, particularly developmental group work, to support learning and social and emotional development in schools.

Two very important themes are woven through the fabric of this report and are intimately connected with supporting learning improvement: the concept of voice and the centrality of girls' friendships. If the *concept of voice* interests you, you may wish to read the following sections together: the right to a voice; assertive voices: the importance of being heard; diminished voices: lack of opportunities for oracy and developing confidence and finding a voice. If you are interested in the *theme of friendship*, you may wish to read the following sections together: equal opportunities, resource distribution and boys' underachievement; learning networks: collaborative and active learning in friendship groups; personal relationship/ friendship difficulties and supporting friendships. feelings about self is also intimately connected with the theme of friendships.

CHAPTER ONE

Rationale and recommendations

The engaged voice must never be fixed and absolute but always changing, always evolving in dialogue with a world beyond itself. (bell hooks, 1994, p11)

Girls are achieving more highly than ever before. Each summer, the newspaper headlines that accompany tears of joy or disappointment as pupils read their exam results tell of another triumph for girls. Their achievement now exceeds that of boys at A level as well as GCSE. Not surprisingly, the public focus is now on boys' under-achievement.

Yet the exam results do not tell the whole story. Girls are still receiving fewer of the resources available to pupils with special needs. This is starkly evident in the complex world of emotional and behaviour difficulty. Typically, boys get more than two thirds of the support available. Assessment procedures that are preoccupied with behaviour rather than emotional need are biased in favour of boys. Girls who are struggling silently with painful emotions, depression, bullying, bereavement or eating disorders are often unnoticed.

A Standards Fund grant allowed a group of teachers and their colleagues in school in Newham to explore ways of supporting girls whose voices had, we felt, sometimes gone unheard. This report records the second year of our project's work.

The action research that forms the basis of this report was conducted by a team of women who are committed to finding new ways of meeting the needs of girls. We recognised that in the rapidly changing world of English schools we need to reflect constantly on our old assumptions and search for new ways of thinking about and pro-viding for girls who are having difficulties in school. Our ideas were developed through dialogue with the girls. It was through con-versation with them, for example, that we learnt how much they appreciated the learning mentors introduced recently into Newham schools.

The team comprised school-based teachers and learning mentors from eight schools; a local authority special needs officer and the head of Newham's Behaviour Support and Tuition Service. The Special Educational Needs Officer and the head of the Behaviour Support and Tuition Service co-ordinated the meetings and communicated between schools. Much valued technical research expertise was pro-vided by Professor Valerie Hey of Brunel University. Valerie joined our team meetings to help us plan the collection and reporting of data and also made visits to schools to support project workers. There was, therefore, a solid connection between the practical work with girls in school and the academic research community.

The new *Code of Practice* gives young people a right to be heard and to be involved in the decisions that affect their lives. This book gives eloquent testimony to girls' perception and insight into the changes schools and teachers could make to improve their experience of and performance at school. By listening we can learn to change lives.

Recommendations: supporting learning and emotional development

The recommendations listed below are directly related to the insights of young women who worked with us in developmental groups over the course of two years. The developmental groups helped us to engage with the young women in finding out about their experiences of school, the organisation of learning and the impact of their social and emotional lives on their learning. They told us schools should create opportunities:

- to engage girls (and all young people) in dialogic ways
- for girls to be heard above the clamour of boys
- to support learning networks
- to do friendship work

Rationale and recommendations

- to learn explicitly from young people about the organisation of school
- to develop social and emotional awareness skills
- to explore and resolve conflict
- to be creative and explore our social and cultural identities

CHAPTER TWO

Rights and wrongs – developments in the policy field

The right to a voice

The right of young people to a voice has been enshrined in social services and health legislation for a number of years. Whilst providers of services, and therefore Local Authorities, have been told to consult with consumers through Quality Protects, The Early Years and Childcare Development Plans and other initiatives, this has not been true of education policy and legislation. The rights of children and young people to have a voice and an active role in decision making and planning in education has, until recently, been particularly lacking.

The issue of the rights of children and young people and their participation in education is a sensitive but slowly emerging area. The recent OfSTED framework *Evaluating Educational Inclusion* places a duty on inspectors to find out from pupils about the organisation of learning within the school by talking directly to them. Recent legislation (*The Special Educational Needs Code of Practice*) has an entire chapter called 'Pupil Participation'. This chapter is about 'the right of children with special educational needs to be involved in making decisions and exercising choices' (DfES, 2001, p27). This chapter begins to articulate some of the difficulties parents may have in seeing children as partners in education. It does not, however, explore the barriers and difficulties that professionals may experience in involving children and young people in decision making. The establishment of the Children and Young People's Unit is also an important step forward. This unit has the task of supporting government ministers as they develop and refine policy and promoting active dialogue and partnership with children and young people. The Economic and

Social Research Council (ESRC) is funding a major project on consulting students about teaching and learning. The project aims to 'integrate a theory of teaching, learning and attainment with a theory of pupil consultation'. Rudduck and Flutter, two researchers involved in the project, argue that 'schools have changed less over the last twenty years or so than young people have changed and many young people struggle to reconcile the often complex relationships and responsibilities of their life out of school with their life in school: in school many young people claim that they continue to be treated like children and they can become increasingly disengaged.'

Wendy Marshall (1996) points out that 'powerful myths of liberal authority' contribute to the absenting of children's power. Further, the way we categorise 'the child' becomes increasingly confused and contradictory as children get older and become young adults.

The historic function of education as social control often prevents practitioners from listening to students' own creative ideas about how systems can change and meet their needs. While many teachers and other adults in schools tirelessly find innovative ways to make sure that their students' voices are heard, strong central government control, including detailed target setting and specification of curriculum content and teaching approaches, hinders students from making choices about their own learning.

The young women with whom we worked felt that they were not treated fairly by adults. Their views were not respected and they were made to feel of less value simply because of their age and their lack of status as young people.

Young people form a historically silenced or muted group in education. We believe that there is a fundamental indignity in speaking for them or on their behalf. Within this commitment, however, we cannot assume that young people have the skills to speak and be listened to and there is a danger of uncritically 'essentialising' their experiences by assuming that they are free to represent their own interests transparently (Spivak, 1988). Thus it is important to engage young people in reflecting on their experiences and enabling them to change unproductive and unsatisfying ways of interacting.

Policy representations of emotional and behavioural difficulties and the social inclusion agenda

Early representations of emotional need are located within definitions of emotional and behavioural difficulties. It is therefore important to trace the construction of the category of the young person with emotional and behavioural difficulties that emerges from policy definitions; to identify how current educational policies continue to prioritise the provision of resources towards boys' emotional and behavioural difficulties and to examine how the category itself functions as a deficit model in which emotional difficulties are pathologised.

Contemporary definitions of emotional and behavioural difficulties originate from the medical deficit model of 'maladjusted' behaviour present in the 1944 Education Act. Subsequent definitions have continued to locate the young person as the problematic source of 'extreme' behaviour that 'causes severe disruption in ordinary schools' (DES, Warnock Report, 1978). The Elton Report highlighted the 'disturbing' behaviour of students with emotional and behavioural difficulties and cited this as a justification for their exclusion from mainstream education:

> A small minority of pupils have such severe and persistent behaviour as a result of emotional, psychological and neurological disturbance that their needs cannot be met in the mainstream schools. (DES, 1989, p150)

In both these texts the focus is on the challenging behaviour of the student with emotional and behavioural difficulties and the 'disturbing' effect of that behaviour in the mainstream classroom. In the context of this report – which drives future policy definitions of emotional and behavioural difficulties – emotional need is identified for a small group of young people, who are pathologised in relation to this need.

In the 1990s, definitions of emotional and behavioural difficulties begin to make specific reference to the socio-cultural contexts within which emotional and behavioural difficulties are located. DfEE circular 9/94 refers to family environments as a possible cause of emotional and behavioural difficulties and recognises that it is not revealed only through acting-out behaviours but that 'emotional and behavioural difficulties may show through withdrawn, depressive, aggressive or self-injurious tendencies'. However, this does not result in an examination of the way in which categories of Special Educational Needs create a notion of the 'normal' student, in relation to which other groups are defined and/or excluded. Also significantly missing from all these definitions is the importance of friendship and the social needs of young people. What we see emerging instead is a wider cultural deficit model that identifies certain social factors such as family as significant in relation to emotional and behavioural difficulties.

Government policies thus appeared to be moving away from deficit constructions towards more social and ecological models of looking at disabling barriers to participation. This led the way for more recent policies, located in discourses of 'risk'. DfEE Circular 10/99 *Social Inclusion: pupil support* identifies a number of groups 'at particular risk', including children from 'families under stress' and pregnant schoolgirls and teenage mothers. The circular points to the fact that family stress can affect young people's emotional and educational development and lists unemployment, bereavement, loss of one or more parents through divorce or separation and new adult partnerships. The circular advises that social services or counselling services may contribute in supporting young people 'at risk'. Similarly, for teenage mothers, the circular advises that schools should work with the LEA and social services. Circular 10/99 identifies young women as being 'at risk' of teenage pregnancy. In the preface to the Social Exclusion Unit report, *Teenage Pregnancy* (1999), the Prime Minister writes: 'I don't believe young people should have sex before they are 16. I have strong views on this. But I also know that no matter how much we may disapprove of them, some do.' Thus the government's agenda of social inclusion continues to trade in deficit models, blame and disapproval. The social inclusion agenda is predetermined and while the government emphasises inclusion, responsibility and citizenship, the social inclusion agenda is not negotiable with young people. Further, young people are now labelled in different ways, reduced to or over-identified with the category of risk with which they are most closely associated. A young woman is, for example, more than just a pregnant schoolgirl and therefore a site of intervention and support; she has the right to dignity and respect and to be seen as more than just her pregnant body. Although this moves on from the process of labelling, the suggestions for support are focused on statutory responsibilities rather than on what young people say they want and need. Following Bradford (2000), these discourses construct certain groups at risk as an essentially problematic social category requiring intervention. Thus government initiatives now locate the problem in whole communities, rather than individual children or their families.

Our project was concerned with situated social practices, voice and participation. Bayley and Haddock (1999) argue for an *interactive* model for understanding emotional and behavioural difficulties that focuses on the set of relationships and classroom processes in the context of the level of skills and the flexibility of support systems within a school. They propose: 'there are some young people who experience multiple social stresses and some of them will experience persistent disturbing feelings and will manifest unusual or bizarre behaviour. The ability of teachers to work with those pupils to provide access to the curriculum is strongly influenced by their perceptions, their level of skills, and the training and support they receive' (p43). Our project therefore focused on situated social practices, enabling young women's participation in an attempt to create flexible systems of support within the school.

It was the organic process of doing the work and listening to the young women that led us to support the move away from the language of Special Educational Needs and discourses of risk that pathologise social and emotional needs. The young women talked about a continuum of social and emotional need that all young people experience. The young women with whom we worked have their own constructions of need, not related to these deficit or socially prescribed models. They identified social and emotional issues for both boys and girls as barriers to learning and participation. They showed an understanding of how challenging behaviours are generated from unresolved emotional issues, how support is often targeted at boys, and they advocated emotional work for all young people.

While acknowledging that the discourses of 'special educational needs' and 'risk' remain part of the policy framework, we believe that they are inherently discriminatory. We share the position outlined in *The Index for Inclusion*: the approach with which these discourses are associated 'has limitations as a way of resolving educational difficulties and can be a barrier to the development of inclusive practice in schools' (Centre for Studies for Inclusive Education, 2000, p13). Integral to the idea of inclusive education is the process of increasing participation and involving students in planning and decision making. The developmental work undertaken in the project involved listening to young women and recording the barriers to learning and participation that they identified.

Equal opportunities, resource distribution and boys' underachievement

Boys' underachievement has had a high media profile recently. The gap in the proportion of boys and girls attaining five or more higher grade passes began to emerge in the 1980s and the debate about boys' underachievement has continued through the 1990s. The 2000 GCSE results allegedly showed girls performed better than boys: 61.1 per cent of girls were awarded a C grade or better compared with 51.9 per cent of boys (Dean, *The Times Educational Supplement*, 15/09/2000). The publication of these results and interpretation of the data resulted in a spate of articles on the issue in *The Times Educational Supplement*. Coinciding with the GSCE results, the then DfEE launched its gender and achievement website in August 2000 with an on-line debate with Michael Barber as to why national figures show that boys fall behind girls in early literacy skills and the gap in attainment widens with age.

Significantly, this debate is not as new as the media or government would have us believe. In an article entitled 'Echoes down the centuries', John Aitken, the headteacher of Keith Grammar School quotes the rector in 1908: 'It is much to be regretted that the proportion of boys to girls in the senior classes of the school should be so small . . . the reason for boys leaving school earlier than girls, and, when they remain, showing less promise, in many cases does not appear to be so much the lack of ability as the absence of earnest endeavour . . .' (*The Times Educational Supplement*, 04/05/2001). If this debate has been around for the last century, the recent fervent attention to boys' underachievement and the attendant emphasis on curricula, examinations and teaching strategies that favour boys' learning must be motivated by something else.

Hey *et al.* analyse the new gender politics of equal opportunity:

> The current discourse of equal opportunity is all about boys needing more help because they are underachieving. This is however framed in by the paradox that boys have in fact always received more resources, albeit that they are said now to need even more because they are not improving as fast as girls. Whereas girls are no longer entitled to attention on the grounds that they (briefly) received some (limited) additional resources, now read as 'more favourable treatment', as a result of feminist activism in the recent past. (1998, p128.)

In all the furore about boys' underachievement, Slater warns that we should not lose sight of the ways in which the girls, supposedly benefiting from better results, enter a society in which they are still likely to find themselves jobless, poorly paid or working for a man (*The Times Educational Supplement*, 08/09/2000). Slater points out that the gap between men and women's salaries has narrowed by just eight percentage points since 1980 and that last year women earned on average thirty per cent less than men. Thus discourses of equal opportunity do not seem to have resulted in *equality of outcome* for girls and women.

Rudduck and Gray caution that 'blanket statements about girls performing better than boys or vice versa are difficult to justify . . . It is important to remember that while gender is one of the key factors affecting educational performance, it functions in relation to other social variables such as social class, ethnic origin and local context.' Myhill (2002) has analysed patterns of classroom interaction in relation to achievement. In analysing the quality (rather than just the quantity) of classroom interactions, she found that the relationship between achievement and gender is complex: 'Whilst it appears to be true that boys do dominate calling out, high achievers dominate positive learning interactions while low achievers dominate more negative classroom interactions' (2002, p347). There needs to be a more

11

sophisticated awareness of the sets of relations that exist between wider social inequalities; local systems of beliefs about learners and learning; schooling cultures and differential achievement' (Hey *et al.* 1998, p140).

Ironically, recent analysis of results suggests that new classroom strategies aimed at improving boys' performance are benefiting girls even more (Henry, *The Times Educational Supplement*, 01/06/2001). Thus it becomes important to consider girls' behaviour and learning styles in an attempt to understand girls' achievement. Girls' networks create informal peer support systems that operate within what Hey *et al.* refer to as the 'masculine orientation which sees learning as sissie' and 'school orientation to support that focuses on behaviour' (1998, p141). These networks paradoxically work to keep formal learning support out and skew resources towards boys.

The issue, therefore, is not about throwing resources at boys or implementing curricula, examinations and strategies that favour boys, but rather about investigating how girls' networks support learning, how the social construction of masculinities operates against a culture of learning, how peer group cultures and their definitions of masculinity and femininity play a part in shaping patterns of achievement, how policies drive learning support that focuses on challenging behaviours, how learning networks operate in schools and how boys are unwilling to seek help from or give help to each other. Targeting resources at girls and understanding how they learn and how their networks operate is a starting point for investigating these questions.

CHAPTER THREE

What we did

Socio-economic background

The London of Borough of Newham sits firmly in London's East End. Traditional industries such as the railways and the docks died in the 1970s and 80s and with their decline came unemployment and poverty. There are signs of recovery. A vigorous regeneration programme is underway. The council is fighting hard – with some success – to reverse the trend of families moving out as soon as they can afford to do so. The transport infrastructure is being developed and there are plans for a major international terminal in Stratford East. The city airport is conveniently based in the dockland area, within sight of the stark new towers of the University of East London. Nevertheless, Newham is still the second most deprived council in the country and the most deprived in London.

The population of the borough is 235,000. Newham has the highest proportion in the country of children under ten. The borough has a rich cultural diversity with over one half of the population belonging to diverse minority ethnic groups. There are also estimated to be between 16,700 and 19,500 refugees and asylum seekers seeking safety in Newham, with significant numbers from Somalia, Eritrea, Uganda, Sri Lanka (Tamils) and Turkey (Kurds).

Issues about structure and organisation of the project

The first phase of Newham's 'Girls with emotional and behavioural difficulties (EBD) Project' ran from April 1999 to April 2000. In this first year teachers from Newham's central Behaviour Support Team were seconded to work on the Girls' Project. Members of this new Girls with EBD Project team worked in pairs in selected schools. Their brief was to establish partnerships with school staff and encourage joint working on initiatives to support girls. In the event, much of the practical work with the girls was carried out by the team members themselves.

In year two, the picture changed. At the outset, the schools' interest in the project was fuelled, at least in part, by a wish to attract extra resources to work with pupils with emotional and behavioural difficulties. In April 2002, at the end of the project's first year, Newham's large Behaviour Support Team was delegated to schools. This move coincided with the establishment of Excellence in Cities in Newham and the then DfEE's decision to pay most of the Social Inclusion Pupil Support Standards Fund grant directly to schools. Schools had more money than ever before to devote to pupils at risk.

The delegation of the Behaviour Support Team meant that there was no longer a central team to run the project, and the additional resources meant that schools were more comfortable about releasing staff to work on the project than they had been in year one. The widespread interest in the first year project report helped to establish a positive climate for the work and we were able to persuade eight schools to release a staff member to develop girls' work in their school. The bulk of the project grant was given to five schools who had not been involved before. The initial schools were given a smaller grant to support the continuation of the work they had already begun.

The aims of the second year were to continue to develop whole school approaches to the identification of, and response to, the needs of girls. We planned to disseminate successful strategies to schools that had not been involved in the initial project and to evaluate and disseminate additional strategies piloted in the second phase. We were able to build on our experience of year one and acknowledge the tensions and ambiguities inherent in the original application. We were, for example, uncomfortable about labelling particular girls as having EBD and limiting our work to a group that had been selected by teachers because of their perceived problems. We recognised that any girl may at some time have emotional or behavioural issues and acknowledged the contextual and interactive nature of emotional difficulties. Our aim was to reach out beyond the special needs discourse. One practical result of this was that girls were encouraged to refer themselves to the project. Groups were not made up entirely of girls whom the schools had already identified as 'trouble' or 'troubled'.

A key aim of the project has been to develop practitioner based research. We wanted teachers to become engaged in action research that illuminated their practice and was of use to them. In the project's first year there was some resistance to the notion of research. Schools were initially suspicious of teachers coming into school to collect data that may have no direct relevance to school development. This uneasiness was greatly reduced in the project's second year, principally because the teachers and learning mentors involved were given time to do the research themselves.

Time is a precious commodity in schools. The relentless pace of the School Improvement Plan, the packed staff meeting agendas, the individual needs of hundreds of children – all these mean that teachers often feel as if they are running as hard as they can simply to stay in the same place. In year two of the Girls' Project we were able to create a reflective and supportive space for the project teachers and learning mentors to meet together and share their ideas and successes. Team members were collectively appreciative of this, although attendance at meetings dropped towards the end of the year when school priorities, including course work deadlines, took precedence.

The meetings were the focus for planning and structuring the project. At the beginning of the year a timetable was prepared showing, for example, when data would need to be collected and reports written. Each school representative prepared an individual action plan, which they shared with staff at school, so that the work was incorporated into school development planning. It was easier to get this done in the second year than it had been in the first because the project team had already established relationships with key staff in school. This process also meant that the work became established in the school. Team members in year one found it hard to end the work with the girls they had come to know well. They did not know whether or not it would carry on. By the end of the second year we were confident that the work was sufficiently embedded in the schools to continue.

CHAPTER FOUR

How we made it work

How much do we wish to see, how much do we wish to understand? What conceptions, and alternative conceptions, of human practices do we have that will enable us to enhance and significantly enrich life and well-being? (Pritchard quoted by Whitehead, 1989)

Participatory action research

Historically, research in education has been done on teachers or to teachers. Research is seen as the realm of experts outside the teaching profession and is controlled by them, giving teachers little or no say in the subject, scope or scale of the investigation and resulting in their alienation from the processes and findings of research. This kind of research often has little relevance or direct benefit to teachers or learners. Action research is controlled by teachers. It aims to improve practice and help develop teachers' professional judgement and expertise. Action research is defined as cycles of planning a change, acting and observing the processes of that change, reflecting on these processes and using these reflections as evidence to inform the next cycle of planning. This kind of research is developmental and helps to embed changes.

Atweh, Kemmis and Weeks (1998) believe that action research has six key features, and that these are at least as important as the self-reflective spirals of planning, acting, observing and reflecting:

- It focuses on the social processes in the classroom and looks at the way pupils relate to each other and the teacher relates to the pupils.

- It is participatory in that it is designed to include colleagues, parents and pupils.
- It is practical and collaborative in that it happens in the classroom and is about changing practice.
- It is emancipatory in that it attempts to change unproductive or unsatisfying ways of working or relating to others.
- It is critical in that the teacher reflects on her practice and tries to become more aware of any constraints embedded in her ways of working and the social relationships in the classroom.
- It is dialectical in the sense that it sets about investigating reality in an attempt to change it; and changing it in order to investigate it.

One of the key issues for the government at the time of writing is to engage teachers in reforming the profession. Teachers have lived through years of reform and centralised initiatives and now want more opportunities to share ideas about learning and effective practice. Teaching is a learning profession and teachers are committed to continuing their own learning throughout their professional lives. Participatory action research enables teachers to become 'pedagogical leaders' in the development and understanding of teaching and learning. If reform is to be driven by the profession, there will need to be more practitioner-based research evidencing the importance of education as a social practice, in which young people learn to engage with social life and to try out and construct identities through negotiation, dialogue and co-operation (Ozga, 2000, p234).

However, if it is to be truly emancipatory, participation in action research must also include learners. We have argued above that one of the challenges to the dominant model of action research is about who controls the agenda. Research agendas can be driven and controlled by various groups, including the government, local education authorities, academics and more recently, teachers; but research agendas do not often involve young people.

The project team has a strong commitment to participatory and emancipatory research agendas that included the young women as co-researchers. We hoped to include young women in the research agenda, as opposed to doing research to them. Young people can engage in research in many different ways. The guiding principle of participatory action research is that it investigates realities (particularly realities that are experienced as oppressive) in order to change them (Atweh *et al.*, 1998). Recommendations about what and how to change can come from children and young people and can be used to inform policy and planning.

Thomas *et al.* argue that 'consistent with the notion of inclusion is the principle that children and young people should be allowed and enabled to determine their own future, and that they should have a say in the way that their schooling proceeds' (1998, p64). They propose that 'if one wants to know what children want, the simple solution is surely to ask them' (1998, p65). This would seem self-evident; schools are not organised in this way, however, operating rather under the principle of 'benevolent paternalism' (Thomas *et al.*, 1998, p65) and the assumption that adults know best. Some young people may not express opinions and ideas in ways that adults find acceptable. It is also the case that some of the opinions and ideas of young people may make adults feel uncomfortable or threatened. It is for adults to analyse and understand these feelings when they are evoked and still operate from the right of young person to a voice. The important question that we were asking during the project is how young people can be *enabled to find their voices and have a say about how the organisation is working*.

There are many creative ways to engage a process of action research for change. Much work has been done in the use of drama, art, writing and play as therapeutic tools, but there is little research in using creative spaces to bring about change. A notable exception is the work of Augusto Boal who has worked to create his Theatre of the Oppressed and is most well known for Forum Theatre. Boal writes:

> Freire talks about the transitivity of true teaching: the teacher is not a person who unloads knowledge . . . the teacher is a person who has a particular area of knowledge, transmits it to the pupil and at the same time, receives another knowledge in return, since the pupil also has his or her own area of knowledge. The least a teacher has to learn from a pupil is how the pupil learns. Pupils are different from one another; they learn differently. Teaching is transitivity. Democracy. Dialogue. (1998, p19)

Following Boal's metaphor of transitivity and intransitivity, we believe that traditionally teaching has been governed by an intransitive relationship in which products are foregrounded over processes and curriculum content is transmitted from the teacher to the pupils. This is not to undermine many teachers' creative initiatives, innovative practices and inclusive processes in the classroom. The National Advisory Committee on Creative and Cultural Education (NACCCE) report states that while there have been many benefits in the intro-duction of the National Curriculum, there are still difficulties in the existing rationale, structure and levels of prescription. The new National Curriculum is skills and outcomes based and there is scope for moving towards transitive teaching that focuses on the processes of learning; but there is a danger that a move in this direction will be increasingly restricted by the cumulative effects of successive changes in structure, organisation and assessment.

Johnson and Hallgarten (2002) argue that the government's proposed changes to the 14–19 curriculum:

> profoundly misreads the workforce needs of employers and the economy, quite apart from any inappropriate weighting of those needs against society's requirements of education. Both employers and society need young people not with more knowledge, but with improved social skills, defined widely. We need oral communication skills. We need interpersonal skills and teamwork. We need better understanding of self, community and society. We need young people who have self-esteem because they have discovered their own creativity and imagination. We need young people who are disciplined and self-disciplined, who can promote the social above the personal.

Johnson and Hallgarten argue further that social education is a very high priority, that teachers are pivotal professionals for national social development and that teachers are best positioned for designing and negotiating this curriculum and pedagogy. Our project – and this book – is an attempt to explore pedagogies that support social and emotional development and to consider how to embed these peda-gogies within a broader curriculum.

Group work and the developmental groups

As the practical accounts of school-based project work in chapter 5 reflect, many different types of groups were used across the project schools: peer mentoring groups, conflict management groups, focused group work around a particular topic or theme, group work shops, circle time groups, outdoor activity based and problem solving groups. Each of these groups could be explored in greater depth. However, one of the preferred techniques that many schools used successfully and that we think is particularly innovative is developmental group work The term 'developmental group work' was used by Thacker and Button at the School of Education, Exeter University to describe the project they ran that investigated developmental group work in primary and middle schools. Circle time developed from this and the Quality Circles approach used by industry. Our own use of the term derives from unpublished training material developed by Jo Robinson. Robinson makes the crucial distinction between the value of activities in and of themselves (the circle time approach) and the developmental groups' use of activities as a vehicle for the processes of reflection, evaluation, action and change.

Drawing on Boal's 'arsenal of the theatre of the oppressed' (1992), which is a set of sensory exercises and games, as well as other games handbooks, we set up small developmental groups, facilitated by project workers. Developmental group work is transitive – the group is the centre of decision-making, dialogue and democracy.

Developmental group work has strong links with the group theory that has become known as circle time. Circle time was originally developed for primary schools but has now been adapted for use in secondary schools. It is a really useful technique promoting social and emotional development. Circle time is typically a model for the whole class – either through PSHE curriculum or delivered during time designated to pastoral development, for example tutor time. It is now being endorsed in the Citizenship education curriculum. Developmental groups are typically smaller. We found that groups of between ten and twelve participants are ideal.

The focus of developmental group work is different from that of circle time. The content of developmental group work, although valuable,

21

is only a vehicle for the processes of reflection, evaluation, action and change. Curry and Bromfield identify the 'conference' as a crucial element of circle time that follows each activity and allows for discussion and evaluation of each subject: 'It is a time to encourage children to offer their ideas, thoughts, feelings and for the teacher to also have an input in order to steer discussion in certain directions if necessary, so that children understand the point of the exercise' (1994, p20). Developmental group work builds on circle time techniques but is much less directive and teacher-led. There is also a far greater focus on reflection and the here and now processes of the group. There is no one point of the exercise other than participating in the group processes, observing the group processes and reflecting on them. Learning is not a one-way process but a democratic process facilitated by shared decision making and dialogue as the group becomes interdependent. There is also a greater focus on feedback (see chapter 9). Developmental group work is aimed at secondary-aged students who are beginning to learn the developmental tasks of higher order thinking skills: the ability to reflect, to learn about learning and to make the social and emotional transition into adulthood.

It is important to note that many of the activities described in circle time literature are appropriate for developmental group work. As we noted above, activities are mostly drama or arts based: an arsenal of sensory and social exercises aimed to wake us up to social, emotional and self-knowledge. A report published in 2001 by the National Advisory Committee on Creative and Cultural Education (NACCCE) recommends:

> There are many ways in schools of enabling young people to discuss and express their feelings and emotions. Among the most important are the arts. (Robinson, 2001, pp36–37)

Some writers and theorists are beginning to look at these as tools for facilitating groups to make decisions and bring about change for themselves. Following Boal, at the heart of our developmental group work was the dual meaning of the word 'act: to perform and to take action' (1998, pxix). The intention in our developmental group work was to create a space that liberates: 'a reflection on reality and a rehearsal for future action' (Boal, 1998, p9).

The origins of developmental group work: T-group theory

The theoretical and operational origins of developmental work can be found in the T-group. The idea for the T-group came directly from the action research and group dynamic theories of Kurt Lewin in the mid 20th century. Following Lewin's action research model, the focus of the group is the use of group dynamics to influence the process of social change and to discover more effective ways of functioning as agents of social change.

Following Shaffer and Galinsky's description (1974), the following is a short description of the key theoretical principles of the T-group – and hence, the developmental group:

Democracy

The T-group emphasises democratic values and an awareness of how cooperation and collaboration facilitate group functioning and impact on organisational structures. Caring for others, being willing to help others and being concerned about the feelings of others are primary learning functions of the T-group.

Learning how to learn, self-knowledge and social awareness

Learning to listen to what others are saying, make careful observations, respond to others and examine the impact of one's own behaviour are all important aims within the T-group. These skills facilitate learning how to learn. Learning how to learn also involves increased self-knowledge by learning in an atmosphere of openness, protected by boundaries of confidentiality: what is said in the group, stays in the group. Another aim of the T-group is to help people become more effective in dealing with others. It provides opportunities for the exchange of emotional feelings in a setting that gives constant feedback about how one is perceived. This leads to greater self-awareness and a greater awareness of the diversity of the needs of others.

Aims of developmental group work

Developmental group work aims to:

- explore the relationship between the individual and her systemic contexts

- examine the acts that link us to others and develop good relationships
- develop social, emotional and self-knowledge
- develop listening and communication skills
- develop empathy and concern for others
- develop confidence and enable participation
- explore and find ways of resolving conflict
- develop the ability to learn how to learn
- explore how young people learn and their views on supporting learning improvement

Supporting the aims of the National Curriculum and global citizenship

The National Curriculum handbook opens with a statement of values, aims and purposes. There are two broad aims listed:

1. The school curriculum should aim to provide opportunities for all pupils to learn and achieve;

2. The school curriculum should aim to promote pupils' spiritual, moral, social and cultural development and prepare all pupils for the opportunities and experiences of life. (1999, p11)

If we are to support the first aim, we need to understand how pupils learn. The second aim gives emphasis to promoting

> pupils' self-esteem and emotional well-being and help[ing] them to form and maintain worthwhile and satisfying relationships, based on respect for themselves and for others, at home, school, work and in the community. It should develop their ability to relate to others and work for the common good. (1999, p11).

Developmental group work provides a method of working with young people to promote the social and emotional skills described above and a way of learning about how pupils learn.

Developmental group work covers many learning objectives of the English attainment targets for speaking and listening. Objective three of the Key Stage 3 and 4 curriculum states that young people should learn to participate as members of various groups. They should be taught to: take different views into account and modify their own

24

views in the light of what others say; take different roles in the organisation, planning and sustaining of groups; help the group to complete its tasks by varying contributions appropriately, clarifying and synthesising others' ideas, taking them forward and building on them to reach conclusions, negotiating consensus or agreeing to differ. Developmental group work also supports the learning objectives of the PSHE and citizenship curricula. The descriptors of breadth of study in PSHE states that young people should have opportunities to develop relationships – for example, by working together in groups; consider social and moral dilemmas and prepare for change – for example, by anticipating problems caused by changing family relationships and friendships. Citizenship education became part of the secondary school curriculum from September 2002. According to the Qualifications and Curriculum Authority, citizenship gives pupils the knowledge, skills and understanding to play an effective role in society but it should also prepare pupils to live their lives in a global society. According to DfEE guidance (circular 09/00), this global dimension to the curriculum includes understanding the importance of social justice, respecting differences and relating these to our common humanity, understanding why conflict is a barrier to development and why there is a need for conflict resolution and the promotion of harmony, and understanding our interdependence on a global scale. In order for the global agenda to become embedded in teaching and learning, there needs to be a more complex understanding of the forms of social learning, including social justice, interdependence and conflict resolution. Developmental groups provide a forum for learning together.

The table in the Appendix explicitly links the aims of developmental group work to the key area of *spiritual, moral, social and cultural development*; and the key skill *working with others*. It explores cross-curricular links to the English, PSHE and citizenship curricula.

CHAPTER FIVE

How schools are making it work

School A

History of the school

School A was founded in 1771 to provide an education for poor girls in the Parish of West Ham. It is the fourth oldest girls' school in England. The school has been linked to early pioneer movements in women's education.

The school population

The school is an 11–16 girls' school. There are eight forms of entry and a total of 1200 students. The school has a staff of 70 teachers and 30 support staff. There are 70 different languages spoken in the school and 44.4 per cent of the girls are eligible for free school meals. Two per cent of pupils have statements of special educational need; the majority of these are for general (12) or specific (6) learning difficulties. Two girls have statements for behaviour difficulties.

Support arrangements in the school

The period 1998–2001 has seen a major change in the way support has been provided for pupils. The school has moved away from offering fragmented support to individual pupils and is developing an integrated approach to include all pupils. Two initiatives have given impetus to and supported this development. Firstly, the LEA delegated the majority of resources from the large, central learning and behaviour support teams to schools in April 2000. Secondly, the Excellence in Cities initiative has provided additional resources for learning mentors who have enabled the school to expand the support programmes available to girls.

In 1998 the school was managing special needs and additional English support well but found the emotional and behavioural needs of girls more challenging. These behaviour needs were largely demonstrated outside the classroom. Staff were aware of high levels of quarrelling amongst girls, disaffection, emotional outbursts, complaints of sickness, absence and anxiety. The three permanent special needs staff felt under pressure. The visiting behaviour support teacher spent only three days per week in the school and concentrated her time on the most demanding cases. There were waiting lists to see the educational psychologist who came in for three days each term.

The school attempted to set up supportive strategies such as peer mentoring. These initiatives had some success but school staff found it difficult to find enough time to manage them effectively. The heads of house were overworked. The school was fortunate in having an informal educator/youth worker on site, who worked tirelessly on extra curricular activities and offered an informal drop-in centre at break and lunchtimes. The school recognised the need for extra provision to meet the needs presented by girls and welcomed the Girls' Project involvement in the school.

School staff report that the Excellence in Cities initiative and the delegation of the behaviour and learning support services have 'made a dramatic difference to our support work. We now have a significant team of workers on the ground. Control is now with the school and is, therefore, tailored to the needs of all the students. We have been able to co-ordinate the English as an Additional Language (EAL), Special Educational Needs (SEN) and Excellence in Cities (EiC) support teams into one whole team working together.'

The team now comprises:

Learning mentors   The provision of learning mentors who are highly qualified in their field has brought a wider range of experience and skills into the school and helped teachers plan programmes that effectively meet the needs of students. In their first four terms, the learning mentors held 552 appointments with students. During this time they dealt with a huge range of issues and discovered students who, unknown to their teachers, were managing great difficulties. The mentors have been able to offer an immediate response to pupils'

28

needs, to mediate with families and to extend links with outside agencies. The success of this initiative means that heads of house have been freed to focus on creating positive experiences for the benefit of all students.

A particularly effective programme initiated by the headteacher and now managed by the learning mentors is the establishment of Diversity Groups. The first groups focused on African-Caribbean pupils who had been identified as an under-achieving group in the school. In the school year 2000–1 a group of underachieving white girls was targeted. There are also Language Groups in the school. Twi speakers, for example, met regularly to discuss aspects of their culture and experience.

The Curriculum Access Team   This newly formed support team works together to support pupils who have learning, language or social and emotional needs.

The Link Centre   Funded by Learning Support Unit money, the Link Centre caters for pupils whose underlying emotional needs inhibit learning. Need may express itself in a variety of ways including:

- unpredictable outburst of behaviour
- attention seeking behaviour
- emotional distress
- withdrawal by absence, truancy, constant sickness or lack of participation
- unexpected traumas including death in the family

The centre provides individual programmes of support. Provision can be made for quiet catch-up time or support in common learning areas or in the classroom. Members of the Curriculum Access Team work with pupils in the centre, setting and monitoring targets and over-seeing individual action plans.

One result of the changes in the delivery of support to girls is more efficient use of outside agencies. There is for example, no longer a waiting list for the educational psychologist and the school is explor-ing new and imaginative ways of using this service.

The Girls' Project

School A was involved in the first year of the project and so had information about the needs and wishes of girls to help inform the planning for the second phase of the project. In their second year staff focused on the issues the girls themselves had identified as important to them.

Primary–secondary transition   The school had been surprised to learn how traumatic the girls had found the move from primary to secondary school. The change was even fresh in the minds of older students. The school already put a great deal of effort into primary links but it was clear from listening to what girls said that more needed to be done. In 2000–1, therefore, the process was reviewed. The initiative was led by a member of the Educational Management Team and supported by the Learning Manager of the Humanities Area.

In that year the school worked much harder to ascertain the views of the students. A simple questionnaire was given to girls to fill in on induction day. They were asked to say what they liked about their primary schools, and their comments were a tribute to their primary teachers. The girls reported that their greatest fear was of being bullied. They were also asked to record anything they would like their tutors to know. Teachers reported that their replies were 'innocent and endearing'. One girl wrote that her mother was dying and this helped staff prepare to manage this situation sensitively when she arrived. Class tutors were able to read this information and build up a personal picture of the girls before they arrived.

Year assemblies took place with the year 7 groups when they arrived in school and this gave staff a chance to make sure that the girls understood the organisation of the school. It was also an opportunity to introduce them to the learning mentors and youth workers. They were also informed about where to go and what to do at lunchtime. A peer mentoring group was organised by trained year 9 pupils and was made available every lunchtime.

This work culminated in a compulsory three day residential for all year 7 students in February at an activity centre in Norfolk. The trip proved very successful and was enjoyed by all the students. Staff had ample opportunity during the three days to begin building supportive friendships for pupils who still appeared to have difficulty establishing relationships with their peers.

For many of these girls this trip was the first time they had been parted from their families. Staff had to spend time with some anxious parents before the event. Some parents were, for example, extremely worried about their girls going near water. The school responded to this and did not schedule any swimming or visits to the beach. One father was so anxious about his daughter that he sent her with large labels sewn onto her coats stating her name and address in case she got lost. Some of the school's pupils come from cultures where they never move around unescorted.

As a result of this work, teachers and support staff now know their year 7 pupils well and are prepared to manage their needs.

Personal self-image   The school recognises that teenage girls are very concerned about their appearance. For teachers, the management of the removal of jewellery and misinterpretations of school uniform are daily challenges. In 1999–2000 the Girls' Project groups highlighted these concerns and talked about how anxieties about appearance can dominate their thoughts and lead to extremes of under-eating or depression. The teacher in charge of food technology chose to tackle this problem by working with groups of students to publicise healthy eating. This was felt to be a positive approach to feeling healthy and good about one's physical appearance. The pupils worked on developing healthy menus and creating posters to be displayed on the wall on the way to the dining room, where they could be read by pupils waiting for their lunch.

The school plans to do more to develop this theme and intends to work with the Physical Education (PE) department to expand the programme to cover exercise next year. The Curriculum Access Team made its own small contribution by holding post-Christmas diet weigh-ins in a room where pupils collect at lunchtime! Another member of the team has begun to run salsa and line dancing clubs once a week.

Conflict management   Many of the girls taking part in the Girls' Project Groups in the previous year found themselves in conflict situations. The school's learning mentors contacted an outside agency to train them in running groups that focus on conflict resolution.

Under representation of Asian girls   It was very apparent that of the girls nominated for involvement in the Girls' Project Groups in 1999–2000, very few were from Asian backgrounds. There are a significant number of Asian pupils in the school and staff were concerned that they were under-represented. It was the staff's experience that, although many Asian pupils do not draw attention to themselves, they often grapple with problems that they internalise. Problems which do surface are often quite severe. The school has experienced difficulties concerning Asian students being picked up by young men in cars at lunchtime. The repercussions for these girls if their families found out could be serious. Other Asian pupils silently carry the burdens of their families until their failure to do their homework or their distressed behaviour brings their problems to light. Teenage Asian girls sometimes find it difficult to negotiate the conflicting cultures of home and school. The headteacher at School A is keen that these pupils are given an opportunity to manage their needs and a learning mentor with relevant experience is being recruited. Teachers have also made contact with an Asian women's support group which is going to work with the school and give advice on providing appropriately for the girls.

In conclusion   Sue East, the Learning Manager of the Curriculum Access Team notes the importance of the project for the school:

> The Girls' Project has been important in that it has given voice to the needs of girls. It has been most interesting to hear the voices of girls in mixed school environments. This comparison has served to reminds us, in a single sex school, that girls in our institutions probably have a louder voice. It was useful last year to be in receipt of an outside view on the needs of our students and the work researched then has successfully furnished the focus of our work this year.

> This year there has been a supportive sharing of good practice which has been very beneficial to the participants in the project. The project has enabled us to measure how we have absorbed the work into the whole school processes.

The project has largely been overtaken by the injection of funding from the EiC initiative. However, this does not detract from the fact that girls have a distinct voice and distinct needs and should attract 50 per cent of the provision available. Well-balanced and emotionally stable women will play a large role in creating a well-balanced society.

School B

History of the school

School B is a large multicultural comprehensive. Examination results at the school have improved steadily over the last nine years. There have been no permanent exclusions from the school since 1995–96. There used to be an all age special school on site for children with moderate learning difficulties. When the roof blew off the school in the storm of 1987 it was housed in School B. This natural event coincided with a political and philosophical move in Newham towards inclusion and the special school became the School B Inclusive Education Unit. In its turn, the unit was replaced by 'resourced provision'. The move was more than a change in name. From then on pupils with special needs were supported in mainstream classes, with access to the full breadth of the curriculum. In 1997 Newham LEA decided that the policy of inclusion was to be developed in all local schools and pupils with moderate learning difficulties were placed in their neighbourhood schools. Pupils on the autistic continuum or with severe communication difficulties continued to have specially resourced places at School B.

The school population

There are currently 1926 pupils on roll, 95 of who have statements. Boys make up 64 per cent of the school population. There are 485 pupils on the SEN register and 44 per cent are eligible for free school meals. Three quarters of the school are from minority ethnic groups and about 50 languages are spoken in the school. English is a second language for 65 per cent of pupils.

Support arrangements in the school

Two important initiatives have influenced the way support is given to pupils at School B. In the summer term 1999 Excellence in Cities funding led to the setting up of a Learning Support Unit and a team of learning mentors. The new initiatives reinforced work on social inclusion already developed by the school. A school inclusion social worker had been recently appointed to liaise between school, home and other agencies. In April 2000 the LEA delegated staff from central teams of the Learning Support Service and Behaviour Support and Tuition Service to schools as a further development in supporting inclusion. As a result there are now nine full-time teachers including the SENCO and four part-time teachers (equivalent to two full-time) in the Learning Support Department with three teachers in the Learning Support Unit (LSU) and Behaviour Support Team. There are 21 learning support assistants (LSAs) and two part-time LSAs based at the school.

School B is a big school, both in terms of numbers of pupils and the size of the site so it is a priority to set up efficient systems of communication. At the beginning of each academic year a special educational needs information pack is distributed to all teachers working with a student so that staff have a quick, accessible overview of all students with SEN. The pack includes a referral form which teachers can use to note any concerns they have about a pupil.

A cross-curricular group which includes teachers in the Learning Support Department and a teacher representative from each subject department meets twice termly and deals with all issues relating to SEN. To assist communication further, each teacher in the Learning Support Department is linked to one or more subject departments and has a particular responsibility for the creation of differentiated materials in their link subject.

Partnership with parents is a high priority for the school as a whole and links are made regularly by pastoral teams, the Learning and Behaviour Support Departments, the Learning Mentor team, the School Inclusion Worker and the Education Welfare Officer. The school runs a weekly after school drop-in surgery for parents unable to make appointments and a monthly coffee morning has recently been organised.

A number of external agencies work with School B and the Learning Support Department to support and promote the progress of pupils with SEN.

The Girls' Project

Transition from primary to secondary school   Two feeder primary schools were targeted for transition work. Initially the SENCOs of both schools were contacted and they identified the girls about whom there was concern. Parental permission was obtained and the girls were interviewed at their primary schools. Most interviews were conducted with girls who were experiencing emotional difficulties. Some of the girls expressed their apprehension about moving to such a large school and had fears of being bullied or of not making friends. They were reassured and told about the programme that had been devised to help them settle smoothly at School B.

The programme consisted of weekly group and individual meetings so students could report their progress in a way they felt comfortable with.

They worked on a 're-tracking' and 'understanding ourselves' scheme of work and had plenty of opportunities to express themselves in the weekly circle time meeting. Girls were asked to reflect on how the programme had helped them:

> I was used to going to a smaller school. I was terrified . . . Girls' group has built up my confidence . . . we do this by getting into a circle.

Another girl wrote:

> I felt scared when we started because I didn't know if I was going to be with someone that I was friends with in primary school . . . I was invited to Girls' Project to sort out my problems.

A third girl wrote:

> Now I don't have that many problems and if I do have problems

I go to my mentor or Ms X. At girls' group I could share my problems.

The school has now strengthened transition links with one particular primary school and has extended the transition scheme to include year 5 as well as year 6 pupils.

Work with NQTs and the year 7 girls' group This group was targeted by the co-ordinator of the Girls' Project. It was supervised by two NQTs and consisted of 30 girls. Fifteen were year 7 girls already involved in the project. Each girl was allowed to bring along a friend.

The aim of this group was to raise achievement by fostering confidence and motivation. Students were involved in planning and leading activities. The group met once a week either at lunchtime or after school depending on the activities scheduled for that week. Activities included assertiveness training through drama, public speaking, discussion forums, basic finance, careers advice, health and beauty, jewellery making, dance, music, ICT and story telling. Rewards were offered to the girls to celebrate their achievement. These took the form of trips to the cinema, theatre, bowling and ice-skating. The school plans to extend the rewards to include residential stays and award nights.

Group and individual work with years 8 to 9 Girls were recommended for the Girls' Project by the heads of year, learning mentors, education welfare officers, the SENCO and heads of school.

Year 8
This group worked on compiling a welcome booklet for new students coming to the school. Girls in this group were very introverted when they started school and they expressed a desire to help the new year 7s. A student mentoring system was set up. Each year 7 was attached to a year 8 girl. The couples met either during scheduled meetings or at break or lunchtime. Both groups of girls expressed a desire to continue meeting after the end of the project.

Year 9
This was a dynamic group of girls who needed both individual meetings and group meetings. Some were very disaffected and welcomed the circle time forum to discuss issues. In it the girls set weekly targets

which were reviewed at the beginning of each session. Girls were asked to bring along any uncompleted class or homework and part of the session was used to catch up with their work.

Attendance and punctuality were an issue with some of the girls in this group and achievable targets were to set to improve those records. To boost their morale, the girls were rewarded for any small achievement.

Attendance and rewards   All girls were monitored on a weekly basis to see if their attendance improved. A theatre trip was planned as a reward for improved attendance.

Future plans   The school plans to set up a girls' space where the girls can go at lunchtime and after school. Transition links with primary schools will continue to be developed.

In conclusion   The Girls' Project had a very positive impact on all the girls in the various groups. In nearly all cases heads of year and subject tutors reported an improvement in behaviour, attitude to work and attendance.

The girls felt that the project was a success because it gave them the forum in which they could voice opinions that they had not been confident about.

School C

History of the school

School C is a large, mixed comprehensive. A new headteacher was appointed in January 2000 and changes are being made. The headteacher and the senior management team recognise that behaviour is linked to both emotional issues and teaching and learning. The school is moving forward and there is recognition that good practice developed in the Girls' Project will have a positive impact for everyone.

Academic performance has improved overall in the last two years. The school has been granted specialist school status for the performing arts.

The school population

School C is a mixed nine-form entry school with a population of about 1339. The majority of the students, 81 per cent, are bilingual and of Muslim and/or Asian background. There are 789 boys and 550 girls at the school. There are 62 pupils with statements of whom 32 per cent are girls. Two of these girls are described as having emotional and behavioural difficulties. Slightly more than half the school population is eligible for free school meals.

Support arrangements in the school

School C, like other Newham secondary schools, has benefited from additional funding through the Excellence in Cities initiative. There are three full-time learning mentors and three part-time learning mentors. One works 0.5 on the Girls' Project, another is a part-time lunchtime supervisor as well as a mentor and the third teaches RE for 0.5 of the week.

The mentors tend to work individually with students but are also involved in some group work. They run an anger management support group and support the Girls' Project in developmental group work.

The school has a Learning Support Unit, called the Student Support Centre. It is staffed by a manager, a full time Learning Support Assistant and mainstream staff for some single lessons. A small girls' group for quiet and withdrawn girls is run at the LSU.

A counsellor from the Child and Family Consultation Service visits the school weekly. Talkshop and the Outreach Service for young Asian women also provide opportunities for counselling in the school. The Youth Awareness Programme and other youth and community workers work in the school through the PSHE programme.

The Learning Support department works with students with emotional difficulties in order to achieve some more equality of provision. The department has worked, for example, with a group of year 9 girls who had become disaffected and were under-achieving. Girls were interviewed individually about their experiences of the school and the findings fed back to the senior management team.

The Girls' Project

The school has been involved in a number of initiatives:

Developmental groups   Girls' groups have been established for girls who have been recommended by the Directors of Study of years 8, 9, 10 and 11. Those targeted are primarily girls with low self-esteem and confidence. Developmental group work for girls in year 7 began in May 2001. Each group consists of eight girls and runs for a ten-week block. A worker from Liveline Express, a counselling service based in Newham, facilitates the groups, alongside two learning mentors who are being trained in developmental group work. The purpose of the group is to raise self-esteem and confidence through the exploration of issues such as self-awareness, friendship, emotions, depression, isolation, bullying and conflict resolution. The group takes place in a circle-time setting. The sessions focus on talking time, to encourage the girls to express themselves. Other activities include role-play, art therapy and games.

One hour a week is devoted to feedback on the sessions between the Liveline Express worker and the two learning mentors. This involves evaluating sessions and planning future work. Any major concerns about the girls are passed onto the relevant Director of Study. Girls evaluate the sessions themselves through a questionnaire after the first five weeks, in order to ascertain areas that need further exploration and identify the activities that they find particularly useful. A final evaluation at the end of the ten-week block assesses whether the girls who have attended have made progress. Some girls have been referred on for mentoring.

Girlspace   Girlspace was established as a space for girls to use at lunchtime. It is situated in a classroom and is open four times a week, on Tuesday and Thursday for years 7 and 8 and on Wednesday and Friday for years 9, 10 and 11. A learning mentor supervises all four days with the assistance of a Learning Support Assistant from Tuesday to Thursday.

Workshop: towards an understanding of the needs of girls   On a recent staff development day the school SENCO and a Learning Mentor led a workshop to help staff explore the impact of girls'

39

emotional needs on their learning. Staff analysed and commented on a case study. The outcome of the exercise was a discussion about the importance of a whole school approach to addressing girls' needs.

Workshops to enable young Asian women to access support services and resources   One of the project's aims was to enable young Asian women to access support services and resources. It was apparent that girls from an Asian background were generally under-represented. Girls often found it difficult to discuss problems because they felt that the conflict between Asian and Western cultures was something that they had to deal with themselves. They felt that staff in general were not able to empathise with them because they might not fully understand how it is to live a life behind cultural barriers. It was evident that a culturally sensitive approach was needed to address issues that affect young Asian women. Agencies such as the Newham Asian Women's Project (NAWP) and the Outreach Counselling Service for Young Asian Women were contacted and several awareness raising workshops were arranged for girls of all years.

NAWP have begun to run lunchtime drop-in sessions at the school twice a week for a six-week period. Girls from Key Stage 3 can use the service on Wednesdays and those from Key Stage 4 on Fridays. Girls are able to discuss any personal issues in a relaxed and informal atmosphere. Those who have attended the sessions have said that they have benefited from discussing their problems with members of NAWP as well as with girls in similar situations as themselves.

In autumn 2001 NAWP also ran several workshops that were more structured and focused on issues including: self-harm, eating disorders, body image, assertiveness and self-esteem and stress management.

Workshops run by the Outreach Counselling Service for Young Asian Women are planned. Several workshops will be running during PSE time, attended by girls who have been recommended by members of staff. Members of Outreach will be able to offer information and advice on mental health issues and support services available to Asian girls. If any girls are referred to the service then arrangements will be made for Outreach to provide counselling sessions during school time and on site.

In conclusion   Staff working on the project in the school report that they found it an enjoyable and rewarding experience. They noted that, as a result of the activities initiated by the project, staff throughout the school began to develop their awareness of the impact of emotional issues on learning. Referrals to Girlspace and the developmental groups increased as more staff recognised their worth. Teachers noticed changes in the girls involved in the project.

Staff working on the project found that there were constraints about working with girls in Key Stage 4. Teachers were reluctant to allow girls to be withdrawn from lessons to participate in girls' groups and although two workshops did run for girls in year 11, this was insufficient time to explore emotional issues effectively. And the girls were reluctant to miss lessons.

School D

School population

School D is a mixed school with 931 pupils on roll, 415 of them girls. There is a high level of casual admissions so the roll is changing constantly and 406 pupils are eligible for free school meals. There are six forms in year 7 and seven forms in years 8 and 9. Sixty-eight pupils have statements, of whom 21 are female.

Support arrangements in the school

The LSU is available in the first instance to students whose attendance is a cause for concern and who may also have experienced emotional or behavioural difficulties. There is one full-time learning mentor who is a qualified social worker. She works in close partnership with parents. Currently she has a caseload of 22 pupils in school. Other pupils have moved to off-site provision. There is also a part-time learning mentor who targets able under-achievers.

The school's behaviour support teachers work with pupils with behaviour difficulties and the LSAs work with pupils with a statement of special educational need and others with specific learning difficulties. Pupils can also be referred to the school counsellor for additional support. Since September 2000 there have been 27 referrals. Five pupils have been referred to the Child and Family Consultation

Service. The educational psychologist is currently working with 14 pupils.

The Girls' Project in the school

The Girls' Project was staffed by a co-ordinator who also had a range of other responsibilities including responsibilities for co-ordinating learning mentors, staff development and five link teachers from years 7, 8 and 10. The team met weekly to discuss projects and pupil progress.

One member of the team attended a session on developmental group work, and two others attended circle time courses. A further member had training in peer mentoring.

The project provided groups to support girls in years 7, 8 and 10 in the school. Year 7 pupils were identified by the SENCO following visits to primary schools. Year 8 pupils were all members of the same tutor group in which poor peer relationships had been identified. Year 10 pupils were all selected because lack of confidence was limiting their potential. New referrals were considered in the context of the groups that had already been established.

Year 7 and 8 groups   Following referral, staff assessed girls' needs by reading files and talking to key staff such as form teachers and the SENCO. Contact sheets were completed after each session to monitor attendance and record the contribution made by each girl. All parents and carers were contacted by post before their daughter joined the project. Parents were also invited to meet the project staff and see the girls' work. Parents were impressed with the project. One parent of a year 8 student herself became involved in the school community project.

Students in years 7 and 8 worked in groups of six to eight and met with their mentor at least once a week. There were three groups in year 7 and one group in year 8. The girls became involved in a range of activities including circle time, individual projects and following up personal issues. One of the main aims for the year was to support identified pupils through primary–secondary transition. Consequently, the first project undertaken by the year 8 group was the production of a booklet called 'Bridges' which contained hints and suggestions for new first year pupils. The second project was a self-awareness display, followed by a presentation evening attended by parents and staff. The display included collage, timelines, desert island music and food. Subsequently, the group undertook a mini-enterprise to raise money for charity. Further projects included the preparation of an assembly for International Women's Day. The group chose to research the life of Anne Frank. The final project for year 8 girls was a community project, again chosen by the girls themselves. They wanted to end the year by doing something to contribute to the school community. At the end of the term, year 7 girls updated the primary–secondary transfer booklet.

Year 10 project One teacher continued the work with year 10s developed in the project's first year. A group of year 10 girls was initially identified by the deputy headteacher in consultation with year staff. The girls selected were perceived to be excellent students who lacked confidence and were not thriving in a whole class setting. The girls expressed a desire to focus on IT skills development as they felt that their uncertainty in this area was undermining their progress. The school allowed the girls to set their own agenda for group meetings and they gained sufficient confidence to speak frankly and clearly about their needs. Sessions were a mixture of circle work and GCSE support work.

In conclusion The delivery team met weekly to share information about the progress of individual students. The Girls' Project facilitators were also asked to report back to the whole staff on the work of the project, in particular the mentoring. Staff conducted and documented interviews with the year 10 girls who participated in the project. The girls commented that the group had helped them become more confident, given them an opportunity to sort out difficulties and helped them get on with other girls. Generally, the staff and girls involved in the groups enjoyed the experience of participating in the projects. There were several indicators of success. The attendance of girls on the project improved and there was good attendance at lunchtime and after-school sessions. Other students (including boys) asked to join in with the projects. A successful mini-enterprise project raised money for charity. The production of the 'Bridges' booklet supported primary and secondary transfer and all the girls were confident enough to take part in assemblies during International Women's Week. Peer relationships improved and there was evidence of the girls in the project giving more support to each other.

School E

History of the school

School E is an 11 to 18 mixed comprehensive. Its small sixth form closed in 2001. The school operates on a split site and has had an increase in roll of 30 per cent from 1999 to 2001. The school came out of special measures in 1995 and the following year Investors in People status was achieved.

School population

The school population is 900 and has a growing imbalance of girls and boys. The incoming year 7 has only 29 per cent girls compared with 38 per cent in the present year 7. There is a wide ethnic mix in the school. The largest group, which comprises 32 per cent of pupils, is Indian. English is an additional language for 90 per cent of pupils and 10 per cent of pupils are refugees. There is a mobility rate of 12.3 per cent and 15.7 per cent of pupils are on the *Code of Practice* stages. Over half the pupils are eligible for free school meals.

Support in the school

The school has a learning support unit and learning mentors funded by the Excellence in Cities programme. A behaviour support teacher works closely with the head of learning support, the SENCO and year heads.

The Girls' Project

The co-ordinator of the Girls' Project is also head of physical education and head of year 9. The aims of the project at School E were as follows:

- to support girls during the transition from year 6 to year 7
- to identify girls needing support within the school
- to respond to issues concerning girls

Year 7 Girls' Group

The main focus of the project was to support girls who were transferring from primary school. The co-ordinator's first task was to identify a group of 13 pupils who would most benefit from extra support, using primary records. Indicators of need used were poor attendance and punctuality, social issues, low self-esteem and behaviour difficulties.

The girls were observed informally during the year 6 Induction Day. This day also provided an opportunity to recognise other vulnerable girls who might not have been highlighted by their primary records. Form tutors supported the co-ordinator with this task by noting any girls who were giving cause for concern. A group of ten girls was finally identified and permission letters sent to parents. They came from eight different primary schools.

The group met once a week for 50 minutes. The sessions were built around developmental group work and a variety of developmental activities took place. A brief evaluation of each session was written. The girls held partner interviews and staff conducted two individual interviews with group members and these provided data for the final evaluation of the group.

The girls were pleased to be invited to join the group. It made them feel special, and they liked being taken out of some of their regular lessons. The group activities were popular, especially the games. During the early sessions group members were finding out about each other. Inevitably perhaps, some pupils were more willing to express their feelings than others. A number of important issues were raised and discussed as the work progressed. Comparing primary to secondary school and good and bad things about their new school were popular topics. The girls were obviously aware that there were considerably more boys than girls in their year group. They felt this 'wasn't fair' and thought the boys might 'take over'. They felt that as there were boys only forms there should also be girls only forms. Eight out of the ten girls said that they would like to be in a girls only form.

The girls noted that in most lessons boys sat and worked with boys and girls with girls. They preferred being and working with other girls. In primary school they felt that there had been more co-operation between the sexes. The girls were concerned with incidents of poor behaviour by boys and felt that when their classes had a 'bad' lesson it was always the boys' fault. However, not all boys were considered poorly behaved and many were judged to be 'OK'.

Generally the girls had felt more secure in their primary schools and they also felt that they had been given more responsibility there. They used to play at break time and lunchtime and this was something they had enjoyed but which did not happen at secondary school. Their main concerns about transferring to secondary school were bullying, homework, new teachers and being late to school

For them the good spaces in the school were IT rooms, the library and the girls' changing room. This was because they were considered to be quiet, clean and tidy and places where you could 'share secrets'. The difficult spaces were the girls' toilets, lining up for lunch and 'lessons where you can't talk'. Lining up for lunch was rated as one of the worst experiences in school because 'you get pushed around'. Good things about being in school included school trips, playing with friends and, for one pupil, 'nothing'. Many of the changes the girls wanted to see were physical changes to the building, for example, fewer stairs, bigger classrooms, and a bigger playground. Some girls wanted different teachers. The lunch arrangements, chewing gum under the tables and bullying were also matters of concern. When asked to discuss factors that stopped girls from learning, all the girls felt that the main factor was 'noisy and stupid boys'. Menstruation and 'some teachers' were also mentioned as contributory factors. Several girls suggested that teachers should put all the noisy children in the same class. They thought that well-behaved children should sit together but found that often this did not happen and that a well-behaved girl was deliberately told by the teacher to sit next to a badly-behaved boy. This was strongly resented.

Being included in the year 7 girls' group was a very positive experience for the girls concerned. But many of those included because of their poor attendance continued to have low attendance rates. Additional involvement with parents may have been of benefit here. By the end of the year, some girls in the group no longer needed the additional support but it was decided to continue it for the others. The project co-ordinator felt that meeting more frequently than once each week would have been an advantage but there were obviously timetable constraints.

Girls' spaces   The co-ordinator recognised the need for some girls' spaces within the school environment. The school is split-site and both playgrounds are dominated by boys playing football or cricket. Girls tend to stand around the edge of the playgrounds or look for opportunities to remain in the building. The situation seemed to be worse in the school's second building where very few indoor activities took place, a classroom was allocated as a quiet space there for year 8 and 9 girls on Wednesday and Friday lunchtimes. No organised activities were planned for these sessions but the number of girls attending each week was recorded. At the end of the project 20 questionnaires were completed.

An analysis of the questionnaires showed that the girls liked the quiet room because it was somewhere they could 'sit down and talk, sit back and relax, have fun, hang out with friends', and 'have some privacy without getting hit by balls'. It was also thought to be a 'warm, peaceful place' and 'the only place to go'. It was definitely a chance to get away from boys. The girls thought that the room could be improved by putting in some computers, posters on the wall, board games, magazines, videos and a television. The idea of more resources being allocated to girls led to the suggestion that there should be a similar space allocated in the main building and the open-ing times should be extended to break times and after school. Some girls wanted their own space in the playground; others wanted girls' talks in school that dealt with subjects like sex and drugs. The idea of having a place to go and discuss problems was also raised. Generally girls wanted the space to be more comfortable, with easy chairs and a drinks machine. A small kitchen was also suggested and 'more interesting decoration'. An average of 25 year 8 girls and 21 year 9 girls used the room each week.

Attendance was always higher when the weather was bad. Most girls used the room on a regular basis although a few dropped in occasionally. Most girls came to the room after they had eaten their lunch and stayed for the rest of the break. Girls who were socially isolated within the year groups tended to make good use of the room. Other activities included completing homework, finishing classwork or simply talking with friends. At the girls' request some stationery including paper, felt tips, glue and scissors were purchased specifically for use in the room. The room was set out as a classroom and did not lend itself easily to certain activities. One year 9 boy asked if he could use the room, because he wanted to sit and read and did not want to play football in the playground. The co-ordinator decided to ask the girls if they had any objections to this and they agreed that this particular boy was 'safe' and could use the room. During the following weeks up to three year 9 boys would regularly come to the room and this caused no problems.

The project identified a clear need for girls to have their own spaces within the school. The co-ordinator recommended to colleagues that the lunchtime space in the second building should continue, and be developed for all year groups and in both school buildings.

Offsite activities   Two offsite activities took place. Ten girls from years 8, 9 and 10 spent an afternoon at a local bowling alley. The girls chosen were identified by year heads and form tutors as pupils who would benefit from social activity of this kind. Several of the girls also made use of the girls' space to write an account of their visit.

These are the accounts by two year 8 pupils:

Pupil 1

> We went to a trip called GX Superball. It was very fun. I enjoyed it, specially when we were playing the game. I felt happy. We wore special shoes which were really comfortable. We did not need to pay. It was free. We wore full school uniform and we went at one o'clock. We travelled on a mini-bus. I had a group. In my group were four other girls. I was the last person to play because my name was typed in last. I got 91 points in the whole game.

Pupil 2

> We went to a trip on the 9th November. We left school at one o'clock. We waited for the minibus to come and pick us up. When

we got there a lady took us to a place and put our names on the board. I was winning. I came second at the end of the game. Then we had to go. I had enjoyed my day out. Ms M had organised the trip. She had done really well.

Fifteen year 9 girls took part in a Girls in Sport convention which was attended by girls from Newham schools where professional coaches presented a programme of sports activities. The girls gave some useful verbal feedback afterwards. They found the introductory talk interesting. It made them feel confident about themselves and about the prospect of the day as a whole and it made them want to take up a sport and aim to look good. They liked being told to 'get their body how they wanted it, not by smoking and not eating, but by finding a sport they enjoyed and eating properly'. Many of the girls particularly enjoyed being in a girls' only environment as some were taught in mixed groups back at school. They wanted to know why there couldn't be more days like this one. They felt that the boys dominated the lessons at school and that most of the boys were bigger and more able than they were and this restricted their full participation in some lessons.

Girls' clubs   The co-ordinator drew on her experience as a PE teacher to work with two student teachers to set up several girls' only sports clubs after school. Clubs were organised for netball, basketball and badminton. Lunchtime football clubs for girls continued to run and their numbers were closely monitored. Because attendance was erratic, staff felt that they might have chosen the wrong activities and planned to start a trampolining club the following term. A cricket team was entered into the girls' league. The lunchtime clubs that continued to run were attended by an average of twelve to fifteen girls.

Following informal and general discussions with girls, it was evident that most did not come from sporting backgrounds and that little emphasis was placed on sport and exercise at home. Two girls who had been active in promoting a dance club/group at school insisted that this be kept from their parents because dancing was not in line with the expectations of their religious group.

Year 10 Geography   There were five GCSE Geography groups in year 10. Two of these were mixed groups, two were boys' groups and one was a girls' group. One aim of the project was to track the progress of these groups with particular emphasis on the progress of the girls' group.

A member of staff expressed concern that some girls in the mixed group were displaying silent and withdrawn behaviour and not participating well in oral work. This raised the question of why girls were having difficulty in finding a voice in the classroom and whether their withdrawal was affecting their achievement.

The co-ordinator planned to observe the group in a lesson which had strong emphasis on oral work. This would be followed by a discussion with the teacher. Target minimum grades and Key Stage 3 results were recorded.

Year 10 reports were written at the end of the autumn term and these were used to monitor the girls' achievements. Target minimum grades were compared to current working grades. Of the eight girls observed, four were on target, one was achieving more highly than expected and three were under-achieving. This outcome was not very different from that of the girls only group. The findings concerned with GCSE Geography were therefore inconclusive and the school concluded that more work needs to be done on the issue. However, the intervention did give the girls' an opportunity to develop strategies to participate and find their voices in the classroom and also allowed the teacher to reflect on her teaching style.

In conclusion It was evident from the girls' comments that they valued the activities provided for them. Most girls felt they had benefited from being part of the group. Membership had helped them to 'stay calm and work better with other pupils'. Some girls felt that they had developed strong friendships in the group. Others reported that they had become more independent as a result of their experiences in the group.

Teachers reported tangible benefits too. The form tutor of one of the girls in the group noted that she had settled in well. Her behaviour was 'good'. There was only one referral in her file for poor behaviour and the expectation of aggressive behaviour had not been fulfilled. These were very positive findings.

School F

History of the school

School F is a Roman Catholic girls' school situated to the north of Newham. The school was founded in 1862 by Ursuline sisters from Belgium. The ethos of the school is rooted in the teaching and traditions of St Angela, the 16th century founder of the Ursuline order. School F was founded to provide Roman Catholic education for girls. It has changed over the past 100 years from a boarding school to a multi-lateral school after the Second World War and now to a Technology College with Beacon status.

The school population

There are 924 girls on roll. A sixth form is shared with a neighbouring boys' school and based at School F. Provision for 11 to 16 year old girls is in year groups of 180 pupils, divided into form groups of about 30. Most year groups consist of six form groups. There are eight forms in year 11. Results for 2001 show that 65 per cent of pupils achieved five or more A to C grades at GCSE. Sixteen pupils have statements of special educational need and a further 16 are at stage 3 or 4 of the *Code of Practice*.

Support in the school

A Curriculum Support Team provides support to pupils on the *Code of Practice* and to those attending the LSU and those in need of support from learning mentors. The co-ordinator of the Girls' Project is based in this team. The team comprises a SENCO and assistant SENCO, three full-time teachers, two teachers who are heads of year of but also work with the Curriculum Support area, an LSU co-ordinator, and two learning mentors. One of the year heads co-ordinates the girls' group and also works in the LSU.

The Girls' Project

Establishing the group The Girls' Project at School F provides support for a group of ten year 9 pupils. The make up of the group is reviewed each term. Activities include parent interviews, one to one counselling and support, quality circle time and outdoor activities.

The girls' progress is monitored carefully. Assessment data collected includes Key Stage 2 SATs scores, Cognitive Ability Test (CAT) scores, predicted SATs, tracking folders, incident sheets, cause for concern sheets, warning forms and records of attendance and punctuality. Girls involved in the project meet weekly with project staff to discuss progress and any other issues the girls wish. There is a fortnightly circle time for group discussion and an off-site activities programme involving problem solving and outdoor events. Consultation with parents/carers consists of meetings and written accounts of proposed activities and progress.

The group gives the girls time to discuss their concerns, time to listen to each other within a structure, time to enjoy shared learning in a different environment and time to explore effective ways of developing their own skills and abilities. The intention of the project is that as the group becomes established the girls will take ownership.

The group co-ordinator selected a group of ten year 9 students as a core for the first girls' group. The number was determined by the costing for Activity Centre groups and the number of pupils plus adults who could be accommodated in the school mini bus. The girls were selected on the basis of incident sheets, cause for concern sheets, underachievement as evidenced in pupil tracking data, form tutor referrals, head of year log, attendance and punctuality data and referrals to outside agencies. A separate brief written profile of each pupil was prepared.

Following the initial selection the project co-ordinator interviewed each girl briefly to gauge their commitment and interest in the girls' group. At this interview the co-ordinator described her ideas for the group, went through the general information about it and discussed what the girls hoped to gain from it. A letter was written to parents/carers and a meeting organised to discuss the outline of the group and to work upon shared objectives.

Long and short-term individual targets were negotiated, based on the information in the monitoring data and pupil profile. Girls were encouraged to set their own targets and these were reviewed formally every term and re-negotiated during the weekly meeting, if necessary.

Outdoor activities were based at the Stubbers Outdoor Education Centre near Upminster, which offered activities including sailing, rock climbing, mountain boarding and problem solving.

The co-ordinator budgeted her time carefully and gave her plan to the senior management team in the school. She was careful to reassure her colleagues that the time of the fortnightly circle time meetings and the weekly individual meetings would be rotated so that girls did not miss the same subject lessons every time.

Development of the girls' work   The girls' group expanded in the summer term, 2001 to include 19 pupils, 11 more than the original group. The catalyst for the expansion was the introduction of a self-esteem project run by one of the school's ex-pupils as part of her final year dissertation for drama. The girls' group formed an obvious nucleus for such work and gave an opportunity to develop the dynamic of the group. The activities for this four-week project were very much in the spirit of the original girls' group. The focus was on attitudes to self-image and alcohol. The girls introduced into the group were composed of girls who

- had overt self-confidence but who were coping with back-ground problems
- had minor problems of peer relationships
- referred themselves

The group was heavily over-subscribed by girls who referred themselves.

The highlight of the expanded group was the trip to the outdoor activity centre. The most surprising members of the group turned out to be the real stars, supporting and encouraging other girls and staff. Both days were successful and every girl expressed her appreciation and hoped to visit again.

The last day of term was very emotional for girls and group co-ordinator alike. The girls were vehement that they wanted the group to continue and delighted that they had had a successful year 9. SATs scores in the school overall were the best ever.

The school believes that this success is in part due to the success of the girls' group in supporting pupils who might otherwise have slipped behind.

The girls' group provided support for girls at risk of not finishing Key Stage 3. The extra time to talk and express their concerns enabled the girls to live through minor scrapes in year 9 and provide support for one another. A noticeable factor was that a setback for one member of the group provided a learning experience for everyone in the group, especially the original members.

Further development of the project   In the first year of the project's life members of the central project team came into school and provided support and opportunities to talk to girls believed to be at risk. This year group continued into year 11 to secure the best ever GCSE passes in the school (69 per cent five or more A* to Cs). The success of the girls' group has led to an expansion in 2001–2. Eight periods have been given to run girls' groups throughout Key Stage 3 in years 7, 8 and 9. Quality circle time is to be incorporated into Key Stage 3 PSE programmes with the girls' group co-ordinator modelling lessons throughout these year groups.

In conclusion   The school has been pleased by the impact the project has had on the school. The head of year 7 reports:

> I have perceived a change in the climate surrounding the girls in the group. I was their year head when they entered the school and I still see them frequently or teach them. I believe that the girls see the group as a way to channel their grievances as opposed to starting a fight. The group has had a calming effect. From the girls that I teach, I consider that they have developed more reasoning skills for dealing with conflict. I am an outsider to the Girls' Project but I know what it is about. I would say that overall there has been a perceptible change for the good.

The girls selected for the group were chosen on the basis of reports of their progress and behaviour in year 8. The head of year 8 notes that 'there have been fewer problems than I would have expected based on my previous experience of year 9 girls'.

The girls' group is now an established, discrete part of the Curriculum Support Department. The co-ordinator of the group records her pleasure at the success of the work:

> Personally, running the group has provided me with an immense sense of achievement. I feel great pride in the girls and in the fact that they have managed to talk their way through setbacks and learned coping mechanisms which will help them, not just through school but in the future. I hope that they will continue to support each other through the coming years.

The Girls' Symposium: celebrating the work of all the schools

The Girls' Symposium was held at East Ham Town Hall in February 2001, to celebrate the work that had been done by all the schools involved during the Girls' Project. The aim was to provide the opportunity for all the girls involved in the Girls' Project to work collaboratively in various workshops, in a pleasant and relaxing environment. Seventy-two girls participated in the event. The theme for the event was self-expression and this was explored in three different areas, poetry, art and drama.

The girls were divided into three groups and worked on a carousel basis, so all had an opportunity to experience the poetry, art and drama workshops. Some excellent work was produced as a result: poems, banners and drama performances. At the end of the day the girls were able to present their work and evaluate the day. It was evident that many felt a sense of achievement and were proud to show their work.

CHAPTER SIX

Girls' perspectives

'Emotional and behavioural difficulties': making sense of the label

Talking with the girls

In the first year of the project we focused, as we have seen, on understanding what the notion of 'emotional and behavioural difficulties' meant to girls and young women in Newham schools. Project teachers spent many hours talking with the girls about what it was like to be a student in a large, London secondary school. The girls demonstrated a rich and complex understanding of their differing and sometimes conflicting positions as daughter, sister, friend (potential) sexual partner – and student. The depth of their understanding might surprise some of their teachers.

Girls' understandings of emotional and behavioural difficulties

Many of the girls we interviewed had a clear perception of how girls' emotional or behavioural difficulties are often located within a physiological deficit model by their teachers. Any difficulties a girl experienced was seen to be the result of something wrong in the girl herself, rather than a response to a complex interaction of influences in the classroom or school.

> . . . with girls, if they have mood swings it's put down to periods or hormones.

Some girls said that if they behaved inappropriately they would be 'sent to medical'; others said they would ask to go, in order to avoid a stressful classroom situation.

> . . . you get all angry or sobby or sometimes you get really quiet and

> can't be bothered – if I want to go to the bathroom and they say no you just go crazy.

The girls with whom we worked had very clear understandings of both emotional and behavioural difficulties and of the relationship between the two:

> I reckon that most boys who are naughty have an emotional problem and they just cover it up with bad behaviour . . . reckon that goes for girls as well.

Girls in mixed schools had significant understanding of the influence of gender on the expression of emotional and behavioural difficulties. They noticed and understood that boys and girls tend to express their distress in different ways and consequently to attract different responses from teachers:

> The teachers here take a lot of interest in the hyper-naughty kids . . . girls' emotions are tried to be dealt with but not their behaviour. With boys they work on their behaviour but not their emotions.

> I reckon that most boys who are naughty have an emotional problem and they just cover it up with bad behaviour. I don't think that most teachers realise it's underneath and just concentrate on their behaviour. I reckon that goes for girls as well.

> Boys don't just sit there and deal with it, they lash out and be naughty and get listened to.

Although the levels of understanding varied, there was a widely held belief that changes in behaviour were a manifestation of underlying emotional problems for both sexes:

> . . . you can always tell, there's always something that they'll do differently . . . they're either really loud, aggressive, moody, or very quiet, don't talk or listen much . . . no-one's ever normal and has problems . . .

Most of our interviewees were able to describe how a girl's behaviour might indicate that she was experiencing emotional difficulties. However, girls were aware that these changes might be quite subtle, or difficult to spot:

> . . . There're signs; they look pale . . . their face changes.

> . . . girls look grumpy . . . their personality changes.

An important finding was that most girls thought it was crucial to have someone to talk to when they needed to.

What stops us learning?

Much of our developmental work involved listening to the girls and recording their voices. They told us explicitly what issues are important to them and how these can be barriers to learning.

Relationship problems

Friendships   The girls were clear that friendship groups are important to them and their emotional well-being. However, when friendships break down they are often left feeling isolated and excluded. This can then lead to mental and/or physical absence from school. Friendship groups are powerful forces in girls' lives.

> Nobody really likes to be alone – it hurts.

> I don't like going to that lesson because X is there and she's always bad to me.

> I didn't want to come to the group at first because X wasn't invited. She is now, so it's okay.

> We worked together as a group when X and Y fell out. It's okay now – they're friends again.

> You can talk to your best friend and not your mum. Without my best friend I can't do things.

Parents   Relationships with parents are also seen as powerful forces in the girls' lives. Positive relationships engendered feelings of well-being and security whereas negative periods in parental relationships could adversely affect the girls. The girls were able to see that being ignored by their parents led to feelings of poor self-worth and could be as damaging as confrontational relationships, if not more so.

> Sometimes my parents don't know whether I'm in the house or not. It feels like they don't care about me.

Doing this group stuff has helped me when I want to talk to my mum.

I talk to my family now. Before I hardly used to talk to them or even look at them . . . but now we make a conversation . . . we get along . . . it's good.

Sometimes I would have problems. My mum would ask me and I would not say anything. I do say something now. I used to get really stressed, get headaches. Now I tell her.

I did not get on with my mother or brother. I used to hate my family . . . I wanted to run away. I understand things better now and I get on with them. Coming to the group has made me realise that your family's the most important thing.

Peer group pressure Whilst peer group pressure can be a positive influence, it is also possible for it to lead to negative outcomes. Girls can feel that they have no choice but to comply with their peer group through fear of becoming an outsider.

I was going to go to my lessons but then X came back to school (after exclusion) so we bunked off together.

We talked about power . . . people taking power from other people – that really got to me. I think a lot of people do that to me and I really realised that.

There are a lot of black girls here. There should be more races. I know a lot of Asian girls would like to come but they can't because of pressure from parents, subjects (homework, coursework, tests etc.) and friends.

Boyfriends Relationships with boys can lead to strong emotional responses from girls. They can feel hurt and confused when relationships break down, and this can undermine their self-confidence and esteem. The girls saw differences in the way that women and men behave in relationships, particularly with regard to openness.

Women constantly make the same mistakes because they trust too much and give too much of themselves. Men lock themselves away and that's why women are always being let down.

You have to keep something for yourself. Women give too much of themselves away.

Women give too much of themselves away because of a lack of self-confidence.

I've got this book called *Women Who Love Too Much*. It's really sad, yeah. They go through their whole life repeating the same process with different men. That's the problem with women.

Love needs to have a limit – we live in dangerous times.

Loss   Loss can take many forms. The girls spoke of losing loved ones – grandparents, parents, siblings and other family members. Some felt this loss through death, others through family separations. Some lost loved ones in traumatic circumstances. All loss had an impact on the girls concerned and affected all areas of their lives.

Even if someone has died you need to keep up a relationship with them and you still feel close to them.

I've got a good relationship with my cousin who is dead.

My dad will always be in my heart even though he's dead.

Academic issues

Transitions   Girls in all the Project schools identified the transition from primary to secondary school as a time of intense pressure. They had been through it themselves and felt that they were not noticed as having problems unless they 'acted out'. They were all keen to reach out to new year 7 pupils, particularly those they perceived as having problems. Some could identify with younger pupils who they saw as having similar problems to themselves at that stage. They noted girls who were friendless, aggressive or lonely or who had weight problems.

Other transition problems concerned moving schools more often than usual, possibly due to family circumstances or to problems at school. This is a point to take into consideration regarding girls who are permanently excluded from school and have the additional hurdle of fitting into another establishment.

It's really scary coming to secondary school. You don't know what to expect.

I feel really sorry for X; she's just like I was in year 7. I've asked Miss A if I can talk to her and help her 'cos I know what she's going through.

I wish we'd had a group like this in year 7; I felt so lonely then.

I wish we could have done something in assembly for the year 7s, to get them to come along at lunchtime, if they were lonely, to talk.

In year 7 I didn't want to come to school . . . I was so wrapped up in my own emotions I didn't care what other people thought . . . I had so many problems.

Lack of opportunity for oracy   Many of the girls felt that boys who acted out took up too much of a teacher's time in class. They felt that they themselves were not listened to and had little opportunity to offer their opinions in lessons. The different levels of personal disclosure between boys and girls also emerged – girls see that boys do not talk about their emotions and feelings as much as girls and this leads to a difference in the way that things are discussed in class. Developmental group work sessions specifically for girls were popular because they felt this gave them the opportunity to have their say.

Boys get more attention because they're naughtier.

Girls open up more. Boys are afraid to show their feelings.

In mixed groups we can't actually talk the way we do now – the boys would probably laugh.

I think the group helped me a lot because I can actually talk to people without being shy. I could not get on with people, I would always be thinking, 'What will other people say or do?'

Since I came to the group I understand that it does not matter who you talk to because everyone is equal, you can talk to everyone.

Pressure to succeed   Many girls said that they were under pressure from schools and parents to achieve academic success. Although they appreciated the need to do their best and do well, they felt that the level of pressure applied was too high. They commented on the amount of subjects that they were required to study – some girls thought they could do better if they weren't stretched so thinly. It was often girls who were more academically able who felt negative about the pressure they were under. Parental expectations were particularly high for girls from certain ethnic backgrounds; others were often aware of this pressure on their classmates. Girls at Key Stage 4 commented on the pressure teachers put them under on GCSE courses. They felt that they had no space to think about where they were going and no time to consolidate their work because of the all-round pressure of the academic curriculum. We found that developmental group work gave them a space in the week where they could voice these concerns and work together to overcome their anxieties.

> I like to come here – it's like an emotional space where we can work things out.

> This year (year 9) I'm really fed up. All the time teachers are coming up to you saying 'You've got your SATs.' I know that . . . it's so much pressure . . . it seems like if you don't pass them it's the end of the world . . . like you'll never get married, you won't get a job . . .

> My family expect me to do well . . . everyone else has. Sometimes it's too much pressure for me.

> Some girls, you know, they're under all this pressure from home. They've got to do well in everything.

> I know that a lot of Asian girls want to come to the group, but can't because they're under a lot of pressure from their parents and subjects.

> School needs to listen more to what we have to say. I needed the space in the group to think and to understand things better. I'm now coping more with my work. Everything's copied up now – do you know, I got an A in my art!

Health issues

Pregnancy   When we asked the girls at the symposium what stopped girls learning, they were clear that pregnancy was an issue. Girls who become pregnant whilst at school tend to drop out of the school system. This could be short term, while they arrange for a termination, or long term, if they decide to keep their baby. They felt that the whole way of looking at schoolgirls who become pregnant needs rethinking.

> If you get pregnant you don't come to school anymore.

> I think she's too embarrassed to come to school now 'cos she's showing.

> X had a baby and she came back for a bit but it didn't work for her.

> I don't really know what happens if you get pregnant. Girls just seem to leave school.

Mental health   The girls felt that mental health issues were a barrier to learning. Many of them identified depression as damaging their ability to take part in school life.

> I get depressed, but nobody listens to me. It makes me feel really low.

> This girl was acting really weird. She's left now – she goes to a special place.

> Depression – that's important. Lots of girls get depressed and there's no one to help.

> Sometimes I feel so down I just want to kill myself. Sometimes I can't think about anything else.

Body image   The girls were aware of issues surrounding eating disorders and self-harm. Some of the girls in the groups had eating problems and even those who did not have an eating disorder were conscious of their body image. Schools were aware of the difficulties but little was done to approach or offer help to the girls. Many of the girls did not enjoy PE and were happy to be able to miss lessons officially. Many would truant specifically from PE. They did not like communal changing rooms, the kit they were required to wear and some of the activities. However, some of the girls liked to do physical activities outside of school.

It's good that I miss PE. I wouldn't go anyway. I go to exercise classes and aerobics out of school.

I don't really mind missing lessons because it's PE – I do like the swimming though.

I don't like dance – you have to wear a leotard.

I didn't want to go to my PE lesson so my friend said to come to the group.

It's upsetting, getting changed in front of everyone and they're all staring at you 'cos you're fat. I'm supposed to be seven and a half stone and have a flat stomach but I ain't. I'd love to wear belly tops but I don't.

Stereotyping

Sexuality Girls saw that society views them in certain ways – this was particularly noted in the magazines they read. Trying to conform to these stereotypes could diminish their self-confidence and esteem, which could in turn lead to feelings of isolation and lack of desire to engage with others.

Girls are just surrounded by make-up – this is how you should look, this is how you should dress . . .

Girls should look tall, thin, voluptuous, blonde, long hair, attractive, nice legs, shapely, busty, sexy, stupid.

It is harder for girls than boys in society because if a girl sleeps around she is labelled . . . all kinds of names. But if a boy sleeps around . . . it gets positive labels.

'Taming' the boys The girls saw that they were being used as a method of social control for the boys in their classes. They saw a difference in the way that boys and girls were treated, even though their behaviours might be similar.

It's like when they put you in mixed groups to work 'cos they think the boys will get on better, not muck about.

Boys are more powerful . . . if a boy is told to sit down he won't . . . boys shout out and put you down like . . . 'you're frigid . . .' it's usually sexual things. If a teacher has more power then you have confidence because you know the boys won't answer back or call out.

Girls have bigger problems but boys get all the help.

They should pay more attention to girls and not just boys because they're just trouble makers . . . just because the boys get sent out the teacher forgets about the lesson.

Sometimes it feels like the teachers are more scared of the boys or something . . . when they muck about they just tell them to shut up, but when it's girls they say, 'I wouldn't expect this of you'.

Domestic responsibilities Many of the girls had responsibilities outside of school that took up a good deal of their time and they felt that their school did not appreciate this. They also felt that they had more responsibilities than boys did and considered this unfair. They saw this continuing in the classroom with teachers asking girls to do tasks that they would not bother the boys with.

I have to be the one boiling the rice and I don't like it . . . no man, it has to stop.

Society is making them (boys) think that they're not supposed to cook.

I have to do the cooking and the cleaning when I get home from school. My brothers don't.

I go to pray every day after school and on Saturdays.

My teacher wanted the classroom cleaned, so he picked four girls for the job.

Reputations The girls were aware of how reputations could easily – and unfairly – be built and become powerful; they could be constructed by other teachers, family members or the wider society. Reputations regarding sexual activity, behaviour, feistiness, moodiness, loudness and so on are negative labels as far as girls are concerned and are often used to exclude them. Some girls felt that the danger of attracting negative labelling was a reason for not speaking to teachers about their difficulties at school.

> I think it is better from someone like you because teachers gossip in the staff room . . . I would not trust any of them . . . there are loads of girls out there with problems. They need solving but they don't do anything about it, but if they come after school or something like that we can help them . . .

> A girl I know has problems . . . all the staff gossip about her . . . a new member of staff learns the girl's name straight away and she had not even met her.

> You have to be one or the other, you can't be in-between. If you are a girl and you don't go out with boys they assume that you are a lesbian.

> At my age people treat you like the plague . . . they are not accepting. It's harder for girls . . . there is a new language for girls – frigid, easy . . .

Emotional issues

Isolation The girls often felt very isolated when dealing with emotional issues. Often they felt that they were the only person in the world experiencing their problems. One of the things that came out of all the groups was the fact that the girls appreciated being in a safe environment where they could talk to others and discover that they were not alone in their worries. This helped them to live with and overcome their concerns and get on with the rest of their lives.

> When I get stressed it's nice to come here and I can relax and talk about things.

> I think they need more people like you and X and set up more of these groups so that people know that there's somebody to speak to about anything.

> I think that group work is good 'cos you're talking to other people and seeing how they feel.

I like all of us getting together. It's nice to know others feel the same.

The teachers here take a lot of interest in the hyper-naughty kids . . . with girls if they have mood swings it's often put down to periods or hormones.

Girls just go quiet and want to be left alone . . . when you've got problems you don't really concentrate.

The girls saw 'being different' as a problem. If a girl could not fit into any group she would be isolated, lonely and unhappy. The difference could be cultural, physical, to do with past experiences, differing abilities or might be perceptible only to the girl concerned. It would isolate them from friendship groups, which the girls saw as being important.

I'd seen them around but they weren't the same as me . . . you see the way people dress, not very good . . . so at first I thought, this group won't work, but then you get to know people and then you think they're the same as you.

At my age people treat you like the plague . . . they're not accepting.

I didn't have any friends but I came to the group and I mixed in with the others.

It's difficult when you don't feel like you fit in – it's lonely when you feel different.

Lack of self-confidence   Lack of self-confidence and self-esteem can make it hard for girls to make their voices heard. Some schools identified groups of girls who were quiet and withdrawn to work with us. This type of work enabled many of them to speak up and voice their worries. They were also able to achieve recognition as valued members of the groups. This enabled the groups to help them over-come their lack of confidence – and this carried over into the class-room.

It's good to know that there are other people. I'm not the only one who has difficulties in school.

I used to be really quiet. I'm speaking up for myself now.

The school would know if I had problems 'cos I'd be quiet.

I was a bit nervous about coming to the group because I thought it meant that I might be in trouble. I thought it was a place for naughty children, to make them straight again. I was glad it was a group thing, not an individual thing.

I think it helped me a lot because I can actually talk to people without being shy. I could not get on with people, I would always be thinking, 'What will other people say or do?'

CHAPTER SEVEN

What girls need to learn and become emotionally healthy people

The girls with whom we worked on the project were clear about what they need so as to have a healthy emotional life and function better in school and at home. Most important was their need to be listened to. They feel that their voices often go unheard and they are not always taken seriously when they state their problems. This is what the girls say they want:

To be listened to

This is what the girls talked about most. The feeling that they went unheard at school and at home was both frustrating and de-motivating – and that could provoke the girls to disruptive behaviour or withdrawal. Because the team members gave them space, both in developmental group work and at the end of project symposium, they were able to tell us their concerns, worries, complaints, dreams, views, ideas and opinions.

> I felt very positive that someone actually cared about my opinion . . . I got to share my opinions with others.

> It made me feel easy about myself, just saying it – saying that I hate my dad. I can say it without feeling guilty.

> It has helped me to be more open. It's helped with my behaviour . . . because someone cares . . . I am now able to voice my opinions.

> Hate is such a powerful word and it comes from deep within. It is good to express it and let out the anger. When you keep stuff in, it hurts so much. I used to do that.

When you're in a group with boys . . . they don't listen at all to you.

Girls like to hold everything inside. I can see that a lot of girls are trying to break out in the group . . . to let their feelings out . . . we still need more time.

Teachers should listen to us more and take on our ideas.

To be heard above the boys

The girls from mixed schools complained that they were often passed over in favour of the boys. This may be due to the disruptive behaviour of some of the boys and the teachers' preoccupation with controlling this behaviour, even if it was at the expense of the girls' education. They felt that in some classes they were taken less seriously than the boys. The girls also felt that they were not treated equally to their brothers in the home. Again, their voices were not heard over the clamour of the boys' demands.

Teachers deal with the boys more because they behave badly.

Boys talk loudly, shout. Girls are more quiet, more aware of getting themselves into trouble than boys.

The boys are naughty, then if they do good work the teachers praise them. If the girls do good work the teachers don't notice . . . they feel girls should do good work all the time.

Girls have bigger problems but boys get all the help because they shout louder.

Sometimes girls are put down more than boys. I don't think people realise how much girls have to go through. When girls are going through their teenage years some people think they are exaggerating. Some men don't understand. They should be told about things because girls are not understood.

Girls have to go through more things, physically and mentally, than boys. Some people just think that a boy can come into your classroom and be rude 'cos that's the way they are – not because they're having problems. A girl can come in and one day she's rude 'cos she's going through boyfriend troubles or she's got problems at home . . .

but it's different for a boy. Boys and girls are treated in different ways.

My brother gets away with everything.

To be treated as equals

The girls felt that adults did not treat them fairly. Their views were not respected and they were made to feel of less value simply because of their age and low status as students/young people. Whilst they recognised the roles that had to be played out in schools, they felt that they were responded to in ways that were not respectful of their place in society as a whole.

In the group we were spoken to by adults on an equal level . . . you could talk to the group leaders about things that you could not really speak to your teachers or parents about.

Teachers need to talk to the girls like equal human beings.

Some teachers don't listen because they think we're young and don't know anything. I know that's not true.

I liked the group leaders. They didn't thrust their opinions on us. They didn't make me feel small; they made me feel grown-up.

I think it's sad that we had to have this group just to voice our opinions. Don't teachers realise that we've got opinions?

Teachers need to talk to us, not at us.

It's the way they (teachers) talk to us. We're not dirt you know.

School needs to listen more to what we've got to say.

To have emotional space

The girls felt a lack of emotional space in school life. They recognised that some problems could not be left at the school gate, but would be with them constantly. Help in resolving these problems was felt to be lacking. The girls also expressed the view that these problems often go unrecognised.

This group should go on because there are girls who've got worse problems than me. I think whoever has the problems should be able to come and join and then we can help them.

Some people hold it in. Everyone should have someone to talk to in life.

Carry on with the groups so that other people can talk to someone if they have problems.

There are times that I am confident and there are times that I falter completely. I am shy and I need a lot of prompting. Someone needs to coax me then I become more assertive again.

There's no space in school for dealing with ourselves.

We needed more time to sit and do the group . . . have a bigger room . . . more space.

If you've got problems they're with you all the time . . . we need space to deal with them.

To have friends

The importance of friendship groups came up time and again in the group work. The girls believed that it was valuable to be able to share both good times and bad with friends. Problems could spill over into school when these groups were disrupted (whether because of school-group changes or if girls within the group fell out). Equally, problems could be averted by the girls working together to help and support each other. This suggests the importance of allowing girls to work within friendship groups and of taking care to place them in known friendship groups when they arrive in year 7.

The difference between being in girls' group and a mixed group is that girls are able to talk to each other more than they can talk to the boys.

Friends are people to share your emotions with.

Someone who understands the way you understand things.

You pick your friends more wisely when you've been hurt.

I like the group because I've made friends . . . they've never been bad to me . . . I always get on with them.

I wished I'd gone to the same school as my friends. I was lonely and I missed them.

My friends are very important to me . . . they give me a lot of support.

I don't like the lessons where they split us up. I like to work with my friends.

At first I was scared . . . they put us with people that I didn't know.

To share problems with each other

The girls emphasised the fact that they needed to be able to share their problems with trusted friends and adults. Some problems could be minimised, or even resolved, by girls themselves working together. Other problems needed to be shared with trusted adults or peer counsellors.

We all listen to each other's opinions . . . we are not selfish . . . wanting to get our opinions out . . . not listening to others.

Sometimes I can work things out when I talk to my friends . . . they help me.

We have peer counselling in the school. It helps some people to be able to speak to them.

In the group we discussed our moods with teachers and how we got into trouble. When I was back in class I would just remember what we talked about and then I could keep quiet. It helped with my lessons.

We did communication skills . . . now I can talk to my family members politer and quieter.

The group leaders are approachable, friendly . . . not wanting to get their job done, get their pay and just walk off.

The girls felt that they were more able than boys to give of themselves. They felt that it was important that they could talk openly about their thoughts, hopes and fears without ridicule or dismissal. It was generally felt that boys were afraid to show their feelings, which they thought was sad for the boys.

We help each other . . . that's important.

Boys don't seem to be able to share their feelings like girls can. I think it's sad for boys . . . they don't get the help.

I think the group helped me a lot. At first I was quiet and shy and I did not know what to say . . . I could not express myself in talking. After a little while of getting to know the others I am more confident.

This is a safe place to talk.

I could not get on with people . . . I would always be thinking, 'What will other people say or do?' Since I have come to this group I understand that it does not matter who you talk to . . . everyone is equal . . . you can talk to everyone.

When my friend started to cry and talk about her problems . . . that came under the category Power. We talked about power. People taking power from people . . . that really got to me. I think a lot of people do that to me and I really realise that.

To be supported by better pastoral systems

Project workers asked the girls if they thought that the school should continue to support them and if so, who they thought best suited to doing this. Their various ideas indicate that flexible arrangements that incorporate both the formal and informal pastoral work in school would be of most benefit. A key factor when working with girls with emotional problems is that they will only talk to the people they feel comfortable with – what works for one girl will not necessarily work for another.

A review of the way in which pastoral systems can help girls with emotional problems should be carried out. Those responsible should have appropriate training, and the value of such work should be recognised by management.

Some girls felt that school staff could continue the work the team were doing and identified potentially suitable scenarios.

- **Form tutors** were seen as the most likely people to pick up on emotional difficulties because they saw the girls more than other teachers. Some girls would be happy to talk to their form tutors, but recognised that they might not have the time. Other girls felt that their particular form tutor would not be a person that they could talk to – either because the tutor was not really interested in work of this kind or because of personality clashes.

- **PSE lessons** were seen by some girls as a possible venue for group work. They felt that the curriculum content of the subject lends itself to this format. The teacher concerned and their attitude towards the work was considered to be the most crucial factor.

- **Subject tutors** were identified as helpful where problems were to do with work.

> My form tutor is nice and we can really talk to her, but not all form tutors are like that.

> Form tutors know more about you than other teachers.

> You could talk to your form tutor about school problems and outside you could talk to somebody about your home problems.

> I think my form tutor could do groups.

> Teachers would have to be interested to do this sort of thing right.

> We could do this sort of work in PSHRE. My teacher's good.

> Some of the things we've done are like PSE topics.

> If you have a problem with a certain subject it's best to talk to that teacher.

Many of the girls wanted work to continue with staff not based in the school, as they felt that they did not want to involve the school in their private problems. Some girls had benefited from the presence of workers from voluntary agencies in school. Girls are aware that there are agencies available to them, but not the breadth or extent of such work. It would be helpful if posters about all the local agencies were prominently displayed in schools for girls to consult. Awareness could also be raised through assemblies, tutor time or PSE. Having drop-in counselling available would be a great advantage. Time should be made available in schools: certain girls are unable to access help outside of school hours. At the time of these interviews learning mentors had not yet been introduced into Newham schools. Girls in the second year of the project valued the support given by these school based but non-teaching staff.

I don't think teachers from the school should do this work because it's not the same.

School counsellors are important to have for more individual talks.

Somebody from out of school would be good because they won't gossip it all round the staff room.

Another teacher should come when you leave. I prefer people from outside the school.

I think we should be able to have one-to-one counselling or group work with outside people to talk to . . . it's difficult to talk to your teachers.

I don't really know who could do this sort of work. I suppose there are other people like you.

CHAPTER EIGHT

Space to talk: how the girls saw the benefits of group work

Chapter 6 explored the barriers to learning as identified by the girls and chapter 7 noted what girls said they needed to help them learn and become emotionally healthy people. In this chapter, we critically consider some of the girls' responses and reflect on the methods we used in our efforts to develop inclusive and participatory processes in our research. This chapter considers the benefits of group work, particularly developmental group work, in supporting learning and pupils' social and emotional development in schools.

Girls were given opportunities to participate in various kinds of groups across the project schools. Developmental group work is one model that was widely, but not exclusively, used. In this section, we identify the different types of groups discussed in the practical accounts given in past chapters and highlight the uses of developmental group work, thus establishing a framework for setting up a developmental group.

Girls talked about how much they valued the chance to be part of a group. Girls repeatedly stated that having opportunities to talk through issues helped them with the process of learning.

Talking about my problems helps me [to learn].

I learned to control myself and talk about my problems with my friends and the teacher.

I haven't found anything difficult. It's all easy going, straight ahead, open, you can say what you want.

I liked everything about the group.

Significantly, many girls with whom we worked said that their primary reasons for coming to school are friendships and learning. The young women identified the interconnectedness of the private spaces of friendship and the public spaces of learning:

> The good things about being in school are education and friends.

> I like being at school because I see my friends and I get on well with my mentor. It would be boring without school. I want to get an education.

> [The good things about school]: Your friends are there. You learn if it is a good lesson. You can speak to a mentor. You get to go on trips.

> I feel sad if my friends aren't at school but then I come to learn so I just go to lessons and get on with my work.

> It's nice to have your friends here, but I come to learn. I've completed all my work.

> The good things about being in the school are the things I like, like Art and Science. I like socialising with friends and teachers.

> The good things about school . . . having friends from primary.

> My friends are here and I can learn more than when I'm at home.

Hey *et al.* argue that when schools are organised to support learning improvement (as opposed to social control or social rescue), an atmosphere is created that helps staff to learn explicitly from pupils about how the organisation is working (1998, p139). In our discussion of equal opportunities, resource distribution and boys' underachievement, we argued that it is important to consider how girls learn in an attempt to understand girls' relative achievement. Developmental Group Work provides an opportunity to support learning improvement by finding out what works for girls.

The benefits of group work, as identified by the girls, are organised under four headings:

- a space where we can explore how we learn
- a space where we can explore barriers to learning

- a space where we can develop social and emotional awareness
- a space where we can have fun and be creative

Two significant themes run across these headings and are intimately connected with supporting learning improvement: the concept of voice and the centrality of girls' friendships.

The concept of voice   Brown and Gilligan's (1992) research work organised around the metaphor of voice proposes that the confident voice of young girlhood is replaced by the diminished and un/voiced self of adolescence. However, Valerie Hey argues that data from her research is more ambiguous, 'representing fragmented and contradictory feminine subjects with contextually variant *assertive* as well as *diminished* voices' (1997, p11, our italics). Following Hey, our findings reveal that girls cite instances of when their assertive voices have made a difference and when they feel that their voices have been diminished by the clamour of boys. They also identified the importance of finding a voice and suggested that developmental group work is one way of supporting girls to find their voices. If the concept of voice interests you, you may wish to read the following sub-sections together: assertive voices: the importance of being heard; diminished voices: lack of opportunities for oracy and developing confidence and finding a voice.

The centrality of girls' friendships   Girls' friendship groups can impact on the learning environment both positively and negatively. At best, girls' friendship groups create networks that support and enable learning. However, the intense and complex world of girls' friendships can operate as an oppositional culture to the culture of learning. Hey argues that a particular group of girls in her research operated a 'timetable determined by their social needs as opposed to the one organised by academic demands' (1997, p77). We refer to this unofficial or hidden 'timetable' devoted to the time that girls spend exploring, analysing and negotiating their friendships, as 'friendship work'. There is evidence of a hidden curriculum of friendship work that either supports or sabotages the national curriculum. If girls' friendships are powerful enough to support their learning or sabotage it, every opportunity should be taken to look at how girls convert learning opportunities into opportunities to do their friendship work and visa versa. If you are interested in this theme, you may wish to read the following sub-sections together: learning networks: collaborative and active learning in friendship groups; personal relationship/friendship difficulties and supporting friendships. Feelings about self is also intimately connected with the theme of friendships. If opportunities were created in school to do friendship work and if lessons were organised around recognising friendships and learning networks, girls might not wish to operate their unofficial timetables and hidden curriculum.

A space where we can explore how we learn

This section demonstrates that it is important to have systems in place that allow exploration of how and why girls are able to benefit from their schools' teaching and learning arrangements.

Learning Networks: collaborative and active learning in friendship groups

Girls consistently recognised the importance of supportive friendship groups that form learning networks. These networks are collaborative and usually formed around friendship groups, converting 'friendship work' into opportunities to learn. When these networks are recognised and used effectively in classroom situations, powerful learning opportunities are created.

School F describes how groups were set up for year 9 girls, in part to support SATs results. A variety of assessment data were used and 'tracked'. Long and short-term individual targets were set and monitored on a weekly basis. Fortnightly circle time for group discussion and an off-site activities programme gave thé girls opportunities to share learning in a different environment, to listen to and learn with each other and to discuss their concerns. School B describes a similar type of intervention with a dynamic group of year 9 girls, some of whom were disaffected. In this group, weekly targets were also set and reviewed. Girls were invited to bring along any incomplete class or homework to the group and rewards were given for any small achievement.

Space to talk: how the girls saw the benefits of group work

Being able to work with people who have shared the same experiences as yourself so they know what you are going through.

I feel happy in my RE lessons because my friend sits next to me. Also in my science lessons because the teacher is nice and all my friends are there, and the classroom is nice – like it's big and spacious and has nice displays.

I feel good when I'm sitting next to someone that I get on with. Even if we do the work, we can have a laugh about it and I feel good at lunchtimes when I'm with my friends.

I like being with my friends and I like most of my lessons. I have an older sister at the school so it is good to have her around.

Assertive voices: the importance of being heard

The young women in our project acknowledged the importance of being heard. They cited instances when they felt that teachers actively listened and 'took their ideas'. Significantly, they linked these opportunities to 'learning better' and to self-esteem and confidence.

In the first year of the project, many girls identified primary–secondary transition as being a difficult time for them. Consequently in the second year, schools tried a number of different interventions to support year 7 girls, enabling them to find their voices and develop confidence. School A asked girls to complete a simple questionnaire during induction day, recording anything they would want their tutors to know. This information was used to target support effectively. Peer mentoring schemes and a residential trip were also planned to support the new entrants. School B focused group work activities around assertiveness through drama, public speaking and discussion forums. School D introduced a 'Bridges' programme that culminated in girls participating in assemblies during International Women's Week. Developmental groups in School E identified spaces in the school as 'safe' and 'difficult' for girls, and looked at the issue of gender imbalance across the year 7 group. Girls' spaces were established as a result.

Learning objectives associated with this work include developing each girl's confidence and responsibility for making the most of her abilities: being aware of and assessing their personal qualities, skills achievements and potential so personal goals can be set and helping girls to acquire a sense of their own identity and present themselves confidently in a range of situations.

I want to make my voice heard!

Girls learn better when they know people listen to them and they know they are worth something. It has been really great to be able to talk and have people that listen and try to help you.

My tutor makes me feel valued because she talks to me and shows interest and concern – some of the other people at school as well, like the people who ran the girls' group, made me feel like my opinions mattered.

If teachers listen to you then you will learn better because you feel good inside and then you can think better.

I am listened to when I need something to happen and my view has changed things. When I was in my English class, my ideas were picked and used above other students.

When we were doing this thing about Storyville, [the teacher] took all my ideas.

It is good to be listened to and to have good relationships with people inside school because if you feel you can't talk to your parents, you can talk to a teacher.

Once I had a problem: I had to miss Science lessons because I had to go to a few Art trips. I really wanted to go the trips so I asked my Art teacher to talk to my Science teacher to come to some arrangement for me. But sometimes I don't speak up because I can't be bothered because I know the reaction I'll get will not be a good one.

Sometimes [my views make a difference]. If I have a problem in my lessons, sometimes I can talk to my teachers and get things sorted out.

The organisation of learning

The girls identified that having their learning styles recognised and learning in a supportive and calm environment has a positive impact on their experience of school.

School C planned a staff development session entitled 'Towards an understanding of the needs of girls' facilitated by the SENCO and learning mentors. The workshop helped to raise the profile of girls' needs and explored the implications for teaching and learning.

Many of the girls commented that they like being supported in lessons and that this helped them to learn. Support teachers and learning mentors can 'broker' relationships with subject teachers and support networks of learning within the classroom.

> Some of the things that help girls to learn are teachers with pictures and stories (use of audio-visual aids) that help you focus.

> There should be music playing in the background in lessons, like in art we sometimes have the radio on in the background like classical or Kiss. I really think it calms students.

> The one thing I liked was having help. It helped me to get along with some teachers.

A space where we can explore barriers to learning

This section explores the psychological, social, emotional, health and institutional barriers to learning.

Feelings about self

The intensely lived personal moments of self-doubt and crises of confidence reflected in the voices below provide a glimpse of how emotional worlds affect relationships and learning. Girls repeatedly describe the 'embodied' effects of these moments and moods: feeling sick, dizziness, stomach cramps. Hey argues: 'My particular reading of embodiment goes further because it also incorporates a recognition of the place of emotions (as material productions) in coercing or seducing as we "make ourselves" into particular subject positions' (1997, p23). Not only do we 'make ourselves' into subject positions, but we are also *made* into subject positions through the 'material production' of emotions. The young woman who 'know[s] that people don't like [her],' the young woman who is concerned about 'being fat' or the powerful poem of the young woman who wishes she were dead are all cases in point. In the first case, the powerful inclusions and exclusions of friendship groups operate to make the young women feel socially defunct. In the second case, cultural, media and local representations/ myths of beauty operate to structure feelings of difference and inadequacy. The feelings articulated in the poem are so powerful and profound that they affect not only the young woman's learning but also her will to live. Developmental group work provides a safe environment to do 'identity work' – to look at how we 'make ourselves' and how we are made into (female) subjects. School C involved a worker from a local counselling service to co-facilitate the developmental groups alongside two learning mentors. The purpose of these groups was to improve girls' self-esteem and confidence through the exploration of these intensely personal feelings. School F expanded the small developmental group to form a larger self-esteem group, facilitated by a former pupil as part of her final year drama dissertation.

Identity work is linked to developing confidence and making the most of our abilities. Learning objectives associated with this work include developing an awareness of and assessing one's personal qualities, skills and achievements; managing praise and criticism, success and failure; recognising influences, pressures and sources of help.

> When I feel unhappy or bad about myself, I keep to myself and [try to] pull myself together. I feel sad, my self-esteem is really low. I've had a nervous breakdown before, in year 8. I had one the other day.

> [I feel] depressed, lonely, sad, angry. I feel sick as well like I get dizzy and I get stomach cramps.

> I know people don't like me but I don't care, but I don't like people telling other people to lie about me.

> Sometimes I feel really unhappy or bad about myself when I feel a bit moody or hear something bad about myself. I think: why have people got to be so bitchy?

Space to talk: how the girls saw the benefits of group work

I walk away from my friends, like on Monday at break times I was so upset so I just sat away on my own. Sometimes I can snap at people. I apologise afterwards but I don't really explain why I was upset because I don't want to bother them with my problems.

I am unhappy when I have no one to talk to and things like that. I cry to myself. I feel left out when I don't go on trips. No one comes to say are you all right. I would like them to come and talk to me.

When I feel bad, I'd like some TLC, a good chat, someone to make me smile, chocolate, diet coke, some space to be alone if I want to be – but really I'd prefer someone to be there to listen to my problems.

Sometimes I worry about my body and being fat, but most of the time I can cope with this. It is every now and then I feel a bit fed up about the way I look. I become quieter and quite sulky – sometimes moody, but it doesn't last that long. [I feel] quite sad, sometimes angry. My friends ask me what is wrong. My mentor asks what's wrong. Most other people don't do anything. Sometimes I need to talk. Sometimes I need to be left alone. I don't know.

Personal relationship/friendship difficulties

Learning objectives associated with relationship work include understanding the changing nature of and pressure on relationships with family and friends, understanding the nature of friendship, negotiating within friendships and recognising that actions have consequences.

The formation and dissolution of friendships are key events in girls' school lives. Girls' friendship groups operate as sites of power and powerlessness in which social norms and differences are constructed and policed. As teachers we have all witnessed the tears and trauma as girls' friendships impact on our classroom routines. What is perhaps surprising is that no spaces have been created in schools to do this friendship work. We argued above that girls will operate a timetable determined by their social needs and a hidden curriculum of friendship work if the learning environment does not accommodate this. This should be read not as a threat but an opportunity to convert friendship and relationship work into learning opportunities and to implement the learning objectives listed above.

Barriers created by personal relationship and friendship difficulties locate young women's subjectivities in a nexus of relationships that impact on their learning and participation and on their discursive position as learner: friend, daughter, (actual or potential) partner in sexual relationships. These subject positions often generate competing or contradictory demands on young women: for example, the young woman who feels 'double' due to the contradictory demands of her relationships with her peers and her family. This 'doubling' is complicated by her relationship with her sister and her 'splitting' into unstable 'good' and 'bad' selves or sub-personalities. The nexus of relationships (with her mother, her sister and her friends) and her confused and unstable constructions of 'good' and 'bad' need unravelling in a safe and supportive context.

Two of the project schools developed initiatives specifically to address the needs of Asian girls. The girls said that they found it difficult to discuss problems because they felt that the differences between Asian and Western cultures are something that they have to deal with themselves. Accordingly School C involved local voluntary Asian women's agencies in the running of lunchtime drop-in sessions, voluntary workshops and school-based counselling sessions. School A recruited a learning mentor specifically with the relevant experience to address the needs of young Asian women.

Developmental group work can explore how these subjectivities are created, the conflicts and competing demands of these subject positions, and how they are negotiated within an institutional setting. Through their constant re-enactment, these positions have become so normalised that we often overlook their significance as, for example, when teachers dismiss or disparage the micro-politics of friendship or the difficulties young women experience in negotiating conflicting identities.

> Relationship with friends can affect girls because when things go wrong and you have to see them in school then it can be really difficult. Life at home and family problems can affect girls because they have got a lot on their minds so that they can't concentrate in school.

Some of the difficult things are when people don't like you and pretend to be your friend.

There are some people that I don't get on with, but if I am having a good day sometimes they spoil it or the teacher spoils it.

Sometimes it is difficult with groups of friends because they argue and get bitchy, but we can usually sort it out. It is horrible when I argue with my friends and I feel left out.

Sometimes my friends can act annoyed by me being hyper. But when I'm normal they like me better. I know that sounds weird . . . with other pupils, I think some of them find me annoying but I don't really know what they are thinking.

Relationships with both family and friends when they're not good ones [affects my learning].

If you have pressure put on you to learn and have friends, and if you have problems with your parents, it makes it hard to learn.

At home I am double. Sometimes I get kicked out of the house. I feel when I be good, I feel bad, like I'm doing a bad deed. When I am bad, I feel good because that's me. Everyone in my generation are angels but I am the opposite – I am the devil. My friends think I am cool and have only got one rule: anywhere I go is a no-smoking zone. If anyone offers me a fag, I'm not going to take it. That's my only rule. Others praise me when I do well. When my mum does the washing up and then she asks my sister to sort the clothes out and she does it. Sometimes I wish I was like her. I swear at her. I feel really bad. I want to be good but you see my sister she is good and when I try to be good, she is better. She does more good deeds. They ignore me and I don't like that.

Health issues affecting young women's learning

Susan Contratto argues that the 'defining moment of adolescence is physical: puberty as an event and as a process is felt in the body in all sorts of complex ways' (1994, p374). Young women repeatedly requested that schools take greater cognisance of the physical and emotional effects of puberty. The Personal, Social and Health

Education curriculum requires that young people develop healthier and safer lifestyles; yet there is an argument to be made that the organisation of schools does not recognise the physical and emotional effects of puberty or manage these in positive ways. Developmental group work provides a forum for such discussions and for schools to learn how they can organise to support young women's physical and emotional changes as well as supporting them in making informed choices about their bodies.

Many of the project schools piloted initiatives to address these issues. School A used the food technology curriculum, working with a group of girls to publicise healthy eating. School C ran workshops focusing on self-harm, eating disorders and body image. Schools E and F piloted 'Girls in sport' and outdoor activities programmes to enable young women to get in touch with their physical selves. However, informal discussions with girls revealed that the majority of girls did not come from families who actively promoted sport and some girls asked that their parents not be informed about their dance club as it was felt that dancing might not be in line with their religious beliefs. Thus the physical and emotional effects of puberty are complicated by the competing social discourses: by contemporary notions about 'healthy bodies' on the one hand, and by social and cultural expectations on the other.

Becoming pregnant was identified by girls as a life event that could affect their education. Newham has a Teenage Pregnancy Project that employs two teachers as prevention and support officers to work with schools in enabling girls to make informed choices about their bodies and to support the continued education of those who became pregnant.

> If girls get pregnant they are messing up their education and then they will never get any good grades and it can be scary for them.

> Depression – if you're depressed, you don't really want to sit in a lesson for an hour. I'm going to do well. I just can't concentrate and that's the time I really need to.

> Health problems like headaches, depression, period pains, feeling tired.

Space to talk: how the girls saw the benefits of group work

> School could be more supportive about girls' medical problems like period pains and mood swings. There could be places in school where you can go to do your work, but not because you've been naughty.

Diminished voices: lack of opportunities for oracy

We argued above that networks are central to how girls organise their learning. Classroom based group work can facilitate these networks, but can also work against the culture of networks when teachers use girls within groupings to control boys' behaviour or when attention is focused on the clamour of boys.

We have also looked at how girls' voices can be both assertive and diminished within the learning environment. However, Hey *et al.* (1998) are concerned that girls often seek to position boys as the despised bearers of deviant social behaviours. It has been argued that girls often position boys in this way in order to comply with social expectations of female docility and goodness. These constructions are used in turn by teachers to control boys' behaviours. Developmental group work creates opportunities to unpack these constructions of girls' docility and goodness versus boys' loudness and naughtiness in a way that helps girls to actively negotiate and construct their roles in the classroom and moves them away from gendered stereotypes of behaviour. A member of staff in School E undertook to investigate why the girls in her Geography group were displaying quiet and withdrawn behaviour and not participating in oral work. Girls were given the opportunity to work through and explore this issue in the context of a lunchtime group. Strategies were developed for dealing assertively with the boys' behaviours and the girls' insights into the teacher's behaviour helped her reflect on her own classroom practice.

Learning objectives associated with this work include becoming aware of the effects of all types of stereotyping and how to challenge stereotyping assertively.

> Being shy or embarrassed. Sometimes boys are so loud in class that it disrupts the class. Some girls are loud too. I'm all right though. Although I am not noisy, I am confident and able to say what I want.

Teachers should be more supportive to girls in lessons. They should realise that girls need to learn and treat them equally – not let the boys take over.

Boys mainly stop girls from learning. They only care about themselves. They can be immature and they're always annoying teachers who have to keep stopping the lessons. A lot of time is wasted.

When the boys are being a pain, well teachers should tell them to stop. It's not really fair on the girls. Why should we not be able to learn because of them?

If I don't know what I am doing, I will ask, but sometimes I am scared to ask . . . Sometimes I don't ask when I am scared.

When girls get help, they learn. If teachers pay more attention . . . if teachers stop the yap, yap, yap then girls will learn.

Teachers should listen to girls more instead of jumping to conclusions.

Listen to me more. Not give so much attention to the kids that play up in class.

The organisation of learning: institutional/systemic barriers

At the heart of education is the relationship between teachers and learners . . . (Robinson, 2001, p101).

The NACCCE report highlights teaching and learning arrangements and discusses the benefits of teaching creatively: 'By teaching creatively, we mean teachers using more imaginative approaches to make learning more interesting' (Robinson, 2001, p102). The report goes on to acknowledge that high levels of prescription in relation to content and teaching methods can have the effect of de-skilling teachers and encouraging conformity and passivity.

An alternative view of the curriculum proposes that it is 'not so much about knowledge to be conveyed, but rather a set of teaching and learning relationships' (Swann, quoted in Thomas *et al.* 1998, p98) in which teacher and learners learn from each other. Interpersonal relationships are crucial in promoting inclusive experiences of learning. In this model, classroom management is understood as part of the broader social processes of the classroom. Behaviours are located in the interaction between teacher and students (or among students themselves) and management of those behaviours must serve the interests of equality of opportunity. When classroom management is constructed as the principal responsibility of the teacher, too much control and an authoritarian climate or too little control and chaos are both possible outcomes.

The balance of classroom management

Too much control

Teachers stop me learning by being so strict.

History, Art and Music are the difficult places . . . In History if I don't get anything right the teacher shouts . . . Art, we are not allowed to walk around . . . I don't like music because I keep on getting into trouble.

Too little control

Some students are really annoying – they tease you and say silly stuff and talk rubbish. They're disruptive in and out of lessons. Sometimes the lessons are boring when students are disruptive. Some teachers are no good at controlling the class.

Teachers don't get involved. They don't stop other pupils from teasing me, but they're more concerned about the lesson. They don't tell the pupils to apologise. I feel let down by my friends because they don't really do anything to support me.

Difficult relationships with teachers

I feel really unhappy in my double science lesson because my teacher's really miserable and that makes me feel miserable and then I start to think about my problems. It's like a morgue in that classroom. I'm not even allowed to speak to my friends.

I don't get on with some of the teachers because of the way they talk to me.

Teachers could be more understanding and patient and not be pushy, angry and impatient which puts me off completely. Teachers shouldn't expect you to know everything so that you don't bother asking any more. Some teachers are understanding and patient and know when you're feeling emotional, others think you're being a pain.

To help girls learn, teachers need to control their mood swings, for example, like PMT. It's nice to come to class and find no animosity against you.

A space where we can develop social and emotional awareness

Among the challenges to education, the NACCCE report identifies a social challenge and a personal challenge. The report states that one of the ways to meet the social challenge would be to 'provide forms of education that enable young people to engage positively and confidently with far-reaching processes of social and cultural change'. One of the ways to meet the personal challenge would be 'to develop the unique capabilities of all young people and to provide a basis on which they can each build lives that are purposeful and fulfilling' (Robinson, 2001, p23).

These two identified challenges can be linked to one of the broad aims of the National Curriculum: to develop spiritual, moral, social and cultural development. The National Curriculum Handbook states: 'Self knowledge, relationships, feelings and emotions are an essential part of the spiritual and moral development of young people.' The Handbook defines self-knowledge as 'an awareness of oneself in terms of thoughts, feelings, emotions, responsibilities, and experiences; a growing understanding and acceptance of individual identity; the development of self respect.' Relationships are defined in the Handbook as: 'recognising and valuing the worth of each individual, developing a sense of community, the ability to build up relationships with others.'

The Handbook suggests that these areas of development can be addressed through the Personal, Social and Health Education Curriculum. However, social and emotional work can be highly sensitive and some young people will need a safer, more intimate context than a (mixed) class of thirty students to develop these abilities. We have already argued that girls' voices can be diminished by the clamour of boys in large mixed groups. There is also a body of research evidence that documents the 'invisibility' of girls through tests of teacher recall. Other spaces must therefore be identified if this vital work is to be carried out with young women in a meaningful way. One of the most powerful interventions that some project schools made through discussions with young women is the creation of girls' spaces, or what School C refers to as 'Girlspace'. School E identified a lunchtime girls' space but also researched 'safe' spaces and 'difficult' spaces in the school buildings in an attempt to make the lived environment friendlier and safer for them. Significantly, these spaces did not remain exclusive or 'separatist' for long – what is important is that girls controlled access to the space.

Developing confidence and finding a voice

We have argued that girls value opportunities to use their voices assertively and resent (sometimes, for complex reasons, colluding with) boys' attempts to dominate or silence them. Having a space to unpack the complex vagaries of voice is important if the girls are to develop confidence and responsibility and make the most of their abilities. Learning objectives associated with this key issue include: developing a sense of their own identity and presenting themselves confidently in a range of situations; becoming aware of how others see them; managing praise and criticism, success and failure in a positive way and being aware of (gendered) stereotyping and able to challenge it assertively.

Schools found many creative ways to support girls in developing their confidence. It could be argued that all the initiatives resulted in increased confidence; however, students mentoring younger girls (School B), assertiveness focused group work (School B) and developmental groups co-facilitated by learning mentors and counsellors (School C) were found to be particularly effective.

> At school I can stick up for myself a bit now and I feel a bit more confident.

> The group has helped me to feel more confident and say things out loud.

> One way being part of the group has helped me to be more relaxed, for example, in little arguments.

I was not very confident – I hardly spoke out. I'm quite bright but that was my only problem.

It has improved my confidence because before, I got nervous about speaking out but now I can speak out a bit more. I got to talk to other students and share similar situations. It was like emotional counselling. And it's been fun too.

If my friends aren't in, then I have to walk alone. I used to get in trouble in year 7. I don't anymore.

It has helped me to grow in confidence and I have made new friends.

It has helped me to grow in confidence and I have learnt about conflict and how it affects me. I am now learning to work with younger pupils.

I liked the group. It was hard at first but then I realised that people will listen to me.

Developing 'emotional intelligence'

Daniel Goleman popularised the ideas of the British psychotherapist, Susie Orbach, who coined the term 'emotional literacy'.[1] Goleman maintains that emotional intelligence is the ability to have empathy, master fear, summon optimism, form good relationships with others and control feelings and impulses. The NACCCE report states:

> Goleman, and many others before him points to the changes and problems that can follow from difficulties in understanding and expressing our emotions. The recent report by the Mental Health Foundation confirms these concerns. (Robinson, 2001, pp36–37)

Following Gardner's work on multiple intelligences, Goleman explored the idea that when young people feel bad about themselves or what is happening in their eco-systemic environments (home, school, the community), they will not be able to learn properly. Brain research has also shown that the integration of the emotional and cognitive centres of the brain is central to learning. In other words, relational and affective development crucially affects our ability to learn. If we are to optimise learning, young people should have environments that nurture and encourage them to develop their potential.

Developmental group work provides a forum for doing this 'emotional work', for developing good relationships, skills of participation and responsible action. Associated learning objectives include understanding the changing nature of, and pressure on, relationships with family; how to negotiate within relationships and recognise that actions have consequences; using the imagination to consider other people's experiences; when and how to make compromises; when and how to seek help.

> It is good to be with other girls and share our thoughts and feelings. It is good to be with a mixed [friendship] group, we can support each other.

> I found it difficult talking about personal stuff like relationships and family because of my experiences. I haven't been around other people my own age very much before I came to this school and I didn't know if the other girls in the group could understand what it is like.

> We talked a lot about emotional stuff. There were lots of discussions. We also did some role-play, some artwork and we played games. We were encouraged to express ourselves.

> We talked about feelings, family, relationships, bullying. We did role-play and acted out different situations; we drew pictures about how we feel.

> Sometimes talking about feelings in front of people was difficult at first. Sometimes when it was your turn in the circle to speak, you had nothing to say.

> There should be more people like learning mentors in the school that you can go to for advice.

Supporting friendships

We have seen what powerful forces friendships are in girls' lives and that their formation and dissolution can affect learning and classroom routines. Not all girls find it easy to make friends however.

Friendship is intimately connected with our need to belong and to self-knowledge and understanding: friends help us to understand who we are. Long (1999) identifies four cornerstones of being a friend: the internal cognitive cornerstone of understanding, the internal emotional cornerstone of empathy and the external behavioural cornerstones of social skills and role taking. For many girls, these cornerstones are learned implicitly through observation and socialisation. For many complex reasons, however, some girls have not learned these skills and need the cornerstones to be made explicit in a safe and supportive environment. School A used the opportunities created by the three-day year 7 residential trip to begin to build supportive friendships for girls who appeared to have difficulty establishing relationships with their peers.

Developmental group work can provide a forum for developing the skills of friendship; but the very nature of the groups themselves create opportunities for friendships through the group norms of caring for others, being willing to help others and being concerned about the feelings of others. Opportunities for emotional give and take in a setting that gives constant feedback about how one is perceived leads to greater self-awareness and a greater awareness of the range of others' needs. Learning objectives associated with this work relate to developing good relationships and understanding the nature of friendship and how to make and keep friends.

> The group has helped me to understand myself and made me work hard and realise that I can be nice and people will like me.

> I've made more friends since I've been in the group. I feel I can talk about personal stuff with both the teacher and the girls in the group.

> I was given the opportunity to be in the group because I did not get along . . . I had problems in school . . . not knowing where things were . . . not knowing much people . . .

> I've met some new people and made some new friends. I've felt like I'm not the only one with problems or that some people are worse off than you are.

> I was asked to join the group because I did not have any friends.

Being able to see your friends because sometimes it's not easy out of school. It's better than staying at home.

I'd like them to listen to me and try to understand, like sometimes my friends can think I'm making a big deal out of something. But they should realise that I'm really upset.

Developing skills in conflict resolution

One of the project workers annotated an interview with a young woman who said that History and Art are her favourite subjects: 'we laughed at this point because there were times at the beginning of the group that this pupil really had problems with the History teacher. She would cry and not be able to do her homework.' Someone in the developmental group helped her with her homework and the group role-played how to approach the teacher, ask for help and manage praise and criticism in a positive way.

When young people are unable to express what they're feeling, they will feel alienated, frightened and angry. These feelings can lead to a range of behaviours that can be disruptive, aggressive, withdrawn and self-harming. Developmental groups can help girls (and all young people) to manage their feelings as well as explore conflict and develop strategies for conflict resolution. Some developmental groups focused on real instances of conflict experienced either in the here-and-now of the group or by group participants in their lives at home, at school, in their peer groups or in the community. Other developmental groups used the forum to offer young women more formal training in conflict resolution. School A contacted a local agency to help learning mentors co-facilitate conflict resolution training and group work. Learning objectives for this work are linked to the citizenship curriculum and relate to the importance of solving conflict fairly.

I learned how to calm down, control our tempers, how to be ourselves. I was always happy to see [project worker].

In the conflict group we also have the space to talk and be listened to. I don't know if my views make a difference, it's hard to say.

It is good to be with other girls and to be trained in conflict. It is good to have space to talk about things and be listened to.

I go to the conflict group. We meet on Mondays, lesson three and look at problems around conflict and how to deal with it. We used to be a big group but recently we were interviewed to see if we want to become workshop leaders and the group is smaller – about ten girls. I am being trained now to do the conflict stuff with year 7. I really enjoy the group. At first it was difficult and the group took a long while to settle down, but now I really enjoy it and I've learnt a lot that I want to pass on to others.

I learn best in my conflict group because I like the way that [the project workers] teach the sessions. It is easier going than lessons and the subject is more interesting. It is more relevant to me.

Dealing with bullying

All schools are now required to have a policy dealing with bullying. Developmental groups can both inform and become a part of that policy. Bullying should be seen in relation to developing confidence and social responsibility. Learning objectives associated with this work are related to understanding the personal and social effects of bullying and how to challenge bullying assertively and safely.

The group helped me with being bullied. They showed me what to do and how to deal with the girls.

When I was younger I was sometimes bullied by older kids. That doesn't happen now.

The group has helped me to deal with bullying a lot better. I've learnt to ignore them and talk about it so that I don't take it out on my family.

The difficult thing about school is getting bullied.

Having fun and being creative

The NACCCE report states that creative and cultural education are not subjects in the curriculum: they are *general functions of education* (Robinson, 2001, p101, our italics). There is much talk of factors affecting motivation and young people's disaffection with the education system. The NACCCE recognises that one of the most effective solutions to the problem of disaffection is to develop active forms of

100

learning that engage the creative energies of young people (Robinson, 2001, p26). Developmental group work can be used to engage creative energies and to re-introduce a sense of fun and excitement into the learning environment. The young women with whom we worked were enthusiastic about the creative activities in the group. The NACCCE report defines creativity and creative activity as being pervasive in the concerns of everyday life. The girls recognise creativity in a more formal sense through dance, making jewellery, drama, art and poetry but also through listening to music, laughing, sharing and talking. Implicit in these definitions is the idea that if the problems of disaffection and motivation are to be addressed, having fun should also be a general function of education.

> We dance, talk about stuff, share secrets, go on trips . . . have a good time and have fun.

> In the girls' group we also do things like make jewellery. We also went to a girls' day at East Ham where we did drama and art and poetry. It was a really good day.

> I also go to 'Girlspace' every Wednesday and Friday at lunchtime. Boys aren't allowed there. My friends and I muck about, listen to music, chat and stuff.

> I also go to 'Girlspace' at lunchtimes. I can just chill out and have a laugh with my friends away from everything else.

Note

1. Emotional Literacy Interest Groups are gaining in popularity. Reva Klein reports in *The Times Educational Supplement* that there is a National Emotional Literacy Interest Group (NELIG) overseeing various local groups. The Southampton Emotional Literacy Interest Group (SELIG) has an online network and cyber-forum for practitioners to share information and ideas (*The Times Educational Supplement* 06/04/01).

CHAPTER NINE

Setting up developmental group work

Setting up a developmental group

Writing a short proposal

If you want to set up a developmental group in your school, first set out your aims in a short, written proposal. Link the proposal to the school's development plan (if possible), social inclusion initiatives and National Curriculum aims and learning outcomes. This could be written in consultation with the PSHE staff, learning mentors or the staff with specific responsibility for pastoral and social inclusion initiatives.

Getting permission

It is essential to get permission for developmental group work. The headteacher and relevant pastoral staff (or staff with responsibility for social inclusion initiatives – including the Special Educational Needs Co-ordinator) should be involved in making the decision to set up a developmental group. It is also important to consult more widely with other colleagues in the school, for example learning mentors, the education welfare officer and the educational psychologist.

It is always important to consult with parents. A parent group may be involved in the decision to set up a group. However, once a group has been identified, write to the parents of the target group, outlining the purpose and aims of the group. Other details of the group should also be given to parents, for example, how often the group will meet, for how long, where and when.

Most significant of all is to get permission from the participants themselves. This is discussed in the section below.

Considering referral processes

No referral process will be without its challenges and difficulties. The implications of the different referral processes should be considered. A school may have a target group in mind for developmental group work. Examples of target groups may be:

- a group in which friendship difficulties are becoming a barrier to learning
- a group of quiet girls who have difficulties participating in whole class groups
- a group of girls who are assertive and whose friendship networks support their learning
- a group in which bullying and/or intimidation is creating difficulties
- a group where attendance in lessons is becoming a cause for concern
- a group who may be offered training in peer mentoring and peer conflict resolution

There are any number of target groups from whom the institution can learn about learning and who may benefit from a developmental group.

If the school identifies a target group, seek to create a group that is inclusive. If participants believe that they have been identified due to some perceived deficit or difficulty, membership of the group may work against self-esteem and the group may over-identify with the difficulty that got them referred in the first place. A variation on the 'sink group' phenomenon may be the outcome. However, in the interests of honesty and democracy, participants should understand how and why they have been identified. This can be a difficult balancing act for the facilitator. One possible solution is to negotiate membership of the group, for instance by inviting target students to choose a friend they would like to bring with them. This has the additional benefit of including students who may have been overlooked by staff: sometimes, students know things about each other of which staff are unaware. Care should be taken that students are fully consulted about participation in the group. If a student does not wish to do so, her decision should be respected.

As in everything, there are advantages and disadvantages in school-controlled referral processes. While it is possible to do specific work around difficulties that are creating barriers to learning, school-controlled referrals can be perceived as unequal and undemocratic, since the students themselves have no control over them.

The most democratic referral process is self-referral. School C in our project created a 'Girlspace' during lunch times (see chapter 5). One advantage of self-referring is that it is controlled by the group participants who make a personal commitment to the developmental group work. One of the difficulties is that it may be harder to maintain a focus for the work and to secure agreement about withdrawal from lessons. Self-referral groups tend to be out of lesson time such as lunch times, breakfast clubs or after school. It may be (but is not necessarily) harder during these times to link the developmental group work to specific learning outcomes.

If the school identifies the difficulty rather than the students, it is possible to set up the group, get the necessary permission and timetable a slot and then ask a larger group (a class or year group) to self-refer to the developmental group. This has the advantage of a democratic referral process in which a focus can be maintained and linked to specific learning outcomes.

Where and when?

It is important to have a room that is large enough for all participants to have space to move about. The furniture should be moveable so that the group can arrange chairs or seat themselves in a circle. It is also important that the room feels safe, comfortable and valued. Classrooms that are easily visible from corridors (through large glass windows) may feel unsafe and dark rooms with no natural light may not be comfortable or welcoming. A room that is in constant use with adults or students walking in and out is also not safe. Schools are busy places, space is limited and conditions are often not ideal, but the space allocated is critical for the success of the group. It is not worth attempting developmental group work in a space that is not valued and does not feel comfortable or safe.

The developmental group meetings can be built into the student's personal timetable. This has the advantage of giving the group status. However, it may also mean that the student is withdrawn from a particular lesson. One solution is to run the groups on a carousel basis so that the same lesson is not missed each week, but the logistics of this become complex in terms of getting permission from or informing staff on a weekly basis. Another idea is to link the developmental group to the PSHE curriculum or another specific curriculum area.

How to do developmental group work

The course or stages of group development

Some students do not find group work easy. Groups change and evolve and not all the phases that groups pass through feel safe for everyone involved. There are many theories of group development, of which Tuckman's (1965) is probably the best known. Tuckman proposes that groups pass through four stages of development: forming, storming, norming and performing. Later a fifth stage of group development was identified: adjourning (Tuckman and Jenson, 1977). The stages are not discrete but rather graduated and incremental, and groups negotiate each stage differently. Barnes *et al.* prefer to think of groups as having certain *developmental tasks* rather than holding a more rigid view of phases moved through and not revisited (1999, p52). The notion of developmental tasks corresponds to our use of the term 'developmental group work'. In chapter 3, we argued that developmental group work has its origins in T-group theory. T-group theory describes two broad phases in the typical course of a group: dependence and interdependence. The following description loosely groups Tuckman's stage theory under the two broader phases of dependence and interdependence.

Dependence In the very early developmental tasks or stages, the participants are likely to feel fairly dependent on the facilitator for providing structure, directing them and keeping them safe. In Tuckman's theory, 'forming' and 'storming' are the two earliest developmental tasks and can be linked with the dependence phase.

Forming is the group's first developmental task. Group members often feel anxious at this stage as they may not know each other, and won't know how they will work together or what the expectations and boundaries of the group will be. Group members are dependent on a facilitator. This developmental task is also affected by how the membership of the group was established: did students choose to join the group themselves, were they invited to do so or were they identified by someone outside of the group? If the latter is true, then group members may have questions or issues about membership of the group. One young woman in our project astutely noted:

> One of my teachers asked if I would like to do the group, but I'm not sure I really had a choice. I wanted to do it anyway.

After an initial phase of dependence, the group is likely to reject the dependence on the facilitator. The group is not at this point *in*dependent of the facilitator, but rather passes through a *counter*-dependence as they begin to try to work things out for themselves. Each participant will attempt to make the group comfortable for herself, which often means behaving in the way she has learnt to react in the group most familiar to her: the family. In Tuckman's theory, this is known as **storming**. This stage is often difficult for the facilitator as it feels as though the group is falling apart. In terms of our focus on *developmental* group work, it is particularly important that the group remains the centre of decision making, dialogue and democracy at this stage. The temptation to try to 'control' the group is strong, but trust in the group is not misplaced and it is very rewarding to see the group beginning to come together and work towards inter-dependence. Storming can, however, also be difficult for some of the group members:

> I found it difficult at first because the group was big and there were some loud girls in there. I also didn't think that the youth workers kept the group in control. As we have got more into the group, it has got better and now we all know each other and listen to each other.

Understanding and negotiating conflict is an expected and important task within the group's development and should not be misunderstood or feared. Personal and group development can often only occur if there is conflict within the group. Barnes *et al.* remind us that 'the social veneer of the nice group masks anger and frustration'

(1999, p71). Groups develop greater honesty and trust through knowing that its members can accept and contain aggressive and angry feelings. The facilitator's task during a conflict within the group is to focus the group on what is happening within it – not to offer solutions but to let the group find its way through the conflict as a developmental task. Obviously, the group's safety (and the safety of each of its members) is paramount and the facilitator may wish to use time out or even to end the session if the safety of the group or any member is threatened.

Interdependence   Once it has negotiated counter-dependence and everyone begins to feel comfortable, the group will start to work together effectively and care for one another. Norms of behaviour will also begin to emerge. Tuckman calls this **norming**. It develops as the group begins to work out roles and responsibilities and the group's patterns of interacting are established. These patterns of behaviour become the norm for the group and each group will make its own norm. Once the norm is established, groups feel much safer and are able to perform on the tasks that have been set.

> When I am here in the group I am happy. I act cool. I feel safe.

> [The project worker] makes me feel comfortable. I feel that I fit in. I can make more friends.

> [The project worker] makes us feel okay.

> In the group, we talk about girls' stuff, like periods, and it's good because it's easy to talk to each other and staff there. You don't feel silly to talk about girls' stuff when you know that others are experiencing the same kinds of things.

> Some of the lessons like PE [are difficult] because there are a lot of discussions in that lesson and I find it difficult to talk in front of certain students – like there are some boys who just take the piss out of everything I say. It was different talking in girls' group because nobody did that.

While all the stages of development (or developmental tasks) are productive and important, **performing** is the stage during which the group begins to work to task. It is important to realise that groups can also return to earlier stages or tasks to re-negotiate difficulties, particularly conflict.

Key operational concepts of developmental group work

The circle   The use of space in developmental group work is very important. Boal notes that the way we use and arrange space is directly related to power. It is useful to think about the typical arrangement of desks in a classroom and what this arrangement tells us about the power relations in that classroom. For example, desks used to be arranged in rows and many classrooms had raised platforms for the teacher's desk. The raised desk that forces pupils to look up at/to the teacher suggests that the teacher is more powerful than the pupils: the figure of authority and custodian of knowledge.

Since developmental group work is about dialogue and democracy, the way the space is used should reflect this. A circle is often used as a symbol of democracy: everyone is equal and has the same status (even the facilitator), and everyone is able to see everyone else. The circle can also foster feeling safe and protected. It is a good idea to reflect with the group about all the things a circle can mean early in the first session. Students usually come up with some good examples of circles in history and in nature. King Arthur's knights of the round table is an obvious one. Another useful example concerns the way that adult buffalo (and other herds of animals) protect and keep their young safe by standing in a circle around them.

Once the group has established and is beginning to perform, it is possible to return to the organisation of space and reflect again about the relationship between space and power. In *Games for actors and non-actors*, Boal outlines the great game of power:

> A table, six chairs and a bottle. First of all, participants are asked to come up one at a time and arrange the objects so as to make one chair become the most powerful object in relation to the other chairs, the table and the bottle. Any of the objects can be moved or placed on top of each other, or on their sides, or whatever, but none of the objects can be removed altogether from the space. The group will run through a great number of variations in the arrangement. (1992, p150)

Next, the students are asked to try to make the most democratic arrangement and to represent the sharing of the power-bottle. Students usually return to the circle as the most democratic arrangement. This game can be used effectively to explore and reflect on the use of space and arrangement of desks in classrooms, classroom management styles and how these are related to teaching and learning styles. The use of the power-bottle is important in reflecting on how much power a teacher should hold, the times when it is most useful to share this power and the times when the teacher needs to hold the power in order to keep the class safe.

Democratic decision making   A key task of the group is to develop *interdependence* and *democratic decision making*. Although the facilitator may need to provide structure and leadership in the early stages of the group's development, she does not have an authoritarian role. Circle time literature explores the idea of the 'waiting game' as way of getting the group's attention in a non-authoritarian way. When the group comes together, the facilitator does not take responsibility for gaining quiet or attention – the group is responsible for its behaviour and norms. One co-operative, democratic technique for gaining the group's attention is to agree a signal. Any participant in the group can use the signal to gain the group's attention, but in the early stages of the group's development, it is usual for the facilitator to model the use of the signal. Robinson writes:

> The leader's (*sic*) waiting must have a quality of nothingness . . . no resignation or martyred patience: all questions and interruptions must be ignored. It must be a non-threatening attitude as well; do not worry about the time you are wasting. It is not being wasted. (Unpublished training material, 1999)

Spect-acting: cycles of acting, observing, reflecting   Boal coins the term 'spect-actor' to describe the combination of the roles of participating and observing. In terms of developmental group work, the participant 'spect-actor' engages in a cycle of acting, observing and reflecting. The cycle for every activity in the group is the same: participants act, observe and reflect on their actions and interactions.

Here and now focus   The learning progress in the developmental group is dependent upon observation of and response to what is occurring in the group itself. We have shown how learning happens from *participating* in the group processes, *observing* the group processes and *reflecting* on them. One of the important differences between early T-group theory and the developmental group is that participants in the T-group are not encouraged to talk about their personal experiences. However, developmental groups do focus on the participants' experiences. The here and now focus should not be lost in these discussions. Thus the facilitator focuses the discussion in the here and now by focusing on the feelings that are generated in the here and now recounting of their experience.

Trust Developmental groups develop the concern of each of the participants for one another, a tolerance of making mistakes, psychological safety and risk taking. Activities designed to build and establish trust are important in the early stages of the group's development. If trust is not established, the group will create norms of behaviour and responses that are shallow and without substance. If trust is not established as a group norm, the group will not feel safe and there will be no disclosure. The group will need to develop trust in each other, in the facilitator and in the group processes.

'Columbian hypnosis' is one activity that can be done when the group is forming and learning about each other:

> One actor holds her palm forward, fingers upright, a few centimetres away from the face of another, who is the hypnotised and must keep her face constantly the same distance from the hand of the hypnotiser . . . The hypnotiser starts with a series of movements of her hand, up and down, right and left, backwards and forwards . . . the partner must contort her body in every way possible to maintain the same distance between face and hand . . . (Boal, 1992, p63)

One of the points of this game is to develop trust, as the hypnotiser is obliged to keep the hypnotised person safe.

The developmental group will slowly build on the trust that is beginning to develop between and among participants. Columbian hypnosis is a simple non-threatening, non-touch game. A game that introduces touch in a non-threatening way is 'leaning-against-each-other' (Boal, 1992, p75): two participants side by side, touching shoulders (the right shoulder of one against the other's left), walk along leaning against one another, each trying to keep her feet as far from the other person's as possible.

It seldom happens that participants betray each other's trust, but this is a possible outcome of trust exercises. If this happens, the facilitator stops the exercise immediately, and the group returns to the circle and reflects on what happened. The point of reflection is not blame – it is to explore how the betrayer and the betrayed feel about what happened and how to protect one another from this happening again. When this does happen in groups, there is usually an underlying source of conflict that would need to be explored.

It is also important to note that some trust exercises will be so difficult for certain participants that they are unable to participate. In the developmental group, no one is compelled to do anything and participants' personal decisions are always given absolute respect.

Disclosure: the primacy of emotion   One of the norms that the group attempts to establish is self-disclosure: revealing one's reactions, feelings and personal responses. This makes the learning process very powerful. However, there is a danger of 'eternal returns' with emotional work: that old ways of feeling, being and behaving are simply reinforced and the participant (or group) remains stuck. If disclosure is to be developmental, it is important to think about how to move personal and group processes forward.

Boal proposes that our senses pick up enormous amounts of sensations and information, but present them selectively to our consciousness. Our bodies are made up of patterns of muscle tissue that form in certain ways because of our routines of moving. Boal calls these processes of selection and structuration *'mechanisation'* and he proposes that emotions run 'the risk of being canalized by the mechanised patterns of the actor's behaviour, the emotion may be blocked by a body already hardened by habit into a certain set of actions and reactions' (1992, p40). Disclosures will not move participants out of old patterns of feeling, being and behaving if they simply rehearse those patterns. New ways of seeing the situation, feeling, being and behaving must be explored. T-group theory calls this 'unfreezing': unfreezing means freeing participants from their standard and typical ways of behaving and of viewing themselves and others in inter-personal situations.

Boal proposes that there are games or exercises that can 'de-mecha-nise' our bodies so that we can learn new ways of feeling, being and behaving: muscular, sensory, memory, imagination and emotion exercises. Simple muscular and sensory exercises are especially useful in the early stages of a group's development. They are also excellent ways of starting developmental group work sessions, as they often energise the participants. A simple, energising and popular muscular exercise is one called slow motion, in which 'the winner is the last person home. Once the race has begun, the actors cannot interrupt their movements which should be executed as slowly as possible' (Boal, 1992, p73). Another simple sensory exercise – and one which also introduces non-threatening touch and builds trust – is 'back writing': this involves the group sitting or standing and a double circle; one person writes a series of numbers or a word on the other's back and the person receiving the sensory message has to say what it is.

Memory, imagination and emotion exercises are usually introduced when the group is beginning to norm and trust has been developed. Exercises that connect memory and emotion can be very powerful, for example remembering a day in the past (Boal, 1992, p162). This exercise can only be done when a group has well developed trust. It can be performed in a double circle or with two individuals. One participant recounts a really important moment in their past – something that made a profound impression, the memory of which provokes emotion even today. This may have a particular theme, such as good memories, difficult memories, memories of oppression etc. Each participant has a 'co-pilot' or supporter who should help the person to link the memory to the sensations by asking lots of questions relating to sensory detail. If this becomes too painful or upsetting, the facilitator might stop the exercise and rehearse a different ending by connecting memory, emotion and imagination. This time the co-pilot may suggest possible actions that might lead to a different conclusion. Everyone uses their imagination to lead the memory to a different, happier conclusion. This is especially effective when remembering instances of conflict between a pupil and teacher, bully and victim, or friends who have fallen out. This is one way of what Boal describes as 'rehearsing for reality': a way of pooling knowledge, tactics and experience to bring difficult situations to a different conclusion so that participants are not stuck in old ways of behaving.

A word of caution: there must necessarily be a limit to how much is revealed since these are developmental and not specialist therapeutic groups. Therefore realistic norms must be negotiated about the degree of self-disclosure that is appropriate to the group.

Feedback   Feedback, or how the participants have responded to each other is one of the most important ways of learning. An honest, straightforward, helpful sharing is encouraged of reactions to and observations about how one's behaviour is affecting others. Giving each other *unconditional positive regard* is one of the key concepts of developmental group work. This does not mean that participants will not provide honest feedback, particularly about behaviours that are unacceptable to the group (for example the betrayal of trust), but it is important that the feedback separates blame and negative indictments of a person from an honest response to the participant's behaviour. This is simply the old rule of 'I like you very much, but I did not like your behaviour just then'.

An excellent feedback game at the forming stage is 'affirmations'. Affirmations can be given in various ways. The 'string connections' game (Robinson, unpublished training material, 2000) works really well in a group to explore our interconnectedness and inter-dependence: one participant starts the game by holding the end of a ball of string and then passing the ball while paying a compliment to another participant, who then keeps hold of the string, passing the ball – along with a compliment – to another participant. At some point, the facilitator briefly interrupts the game and asks the group to reflect on what will happen at the end of the game. Participants are quick to acknowledge that someone will be the last to be offered the ball of string. The facilitator asks how this person might feel and then asks the group to solve this difficulty. Groups have very creative ways of doing this. At the end of the activity, while still holding the string, the group reflects on the game and on the 'string connections' as a metaphor for our interdependence.

Another very successful feedback game is to provide affirmations written on pieces of card. These are laid out in the centre of the circle and participants are asked to choose one for themselves. They are then asked to give out affirmations to each other – as many as they like. The facilitator asks the group how they will take care of each other and make sure that everyone is given at least one affirmation.

The roles of the facilitator

It is stating the obvious to note that schools are busy places and timetables are very full. However, as the process of inclusion develops, it is not uncommon to have two practitioners in a classroom together. Some schools in our project employed co-facilitators from outside agencies. In a classroom, it is usual for one practitioner to lead the group while another acts in a supporting role. While we recognise that groups can be successfully facilitated by one person, we found that best practice is to have two facilitators in a group: one providing the structure (in the early stages of the group) and the other in a support role of participant–observer. In the early stages of the group (forming and storming), facilitating the group can be demanding and stressful. The function of observing group processes and the interaction between and among participants is crucial and this can get lost if there is only one facilitator. So the roles of lead-facilitator and participant–observer must be shared, at least in these early stages. We found that fascinating learning opportunities are created when the roles of lead-facilitator and participant–observer are swapped occasionally.

Facilitating learning The facilitator must be able to create an atmosphere for effective learning. This is a difficult job. It involves setting the scene, making clear that she sees herself as a group member and participant and not as a figure of authority. She will help the group develop its own norms but will not impose those norms. She will model desired behaviours and norms, such as openness, honesty and responsiveness to the needs of others. The facilitator does not manipulate or influence the group. She explains the activities but in complete acceptance that the group might alter them.

Keeping the group safe – discussing confidentiality and monitoring group processes   One of the most important roles of the facilitator is to keep everyone safe. Developing an atmosphere of trust is one way of doing this. Part of feeling safe and being able to trust is about feeling confident that what is said in the group stays in the group. Thus the facilitator will discuss with the group the rules of confidentiality. It is very important that adult participants also respect this rule. As one young woman said:

> [During difficult times] I would like people to speak to me and have one-to-one conversations – if it's confidential: keep the information to themselves and not go spreading it.

As we proposed above, one of the group norms is personal disclosure; however, there must be a limit to how much is revealed. We proposed that realistic norms must be negotiated about the degree of self-disclosure that is appropriate to the group. The facilitator should also plan for disclosure that may not be appropriate and how to handle such instances, including referrals to other agencies. The facilitator should be familiar with child protection regulations and procedures. It is good practice to discuss the nature and operations of the developmental groups as well as referrals to the group with the school's Child Protection Officer prior to starting group work.

Another important way of keeping the group safe is the vigilant monitoring of group processes by carefully observing interactions between participants. As already suggested, best practice is for a participant–observer to assume this role, at least in the early stages of the group's development. The facilitator deflects non-constructive or negative feedback between participants. The facilitator also keeps the group focused on group processes, increasingly enabling the group participants to give each other productive feedback.

The group may need the facilitator to provide structure in the earlier stages but she will work towards letting this responsibility and control go as the group begins to establish its own path of development.

Balancing roles: animateur, enabler, member, joker   The French word *animateur* captures the complex intricacies of the role of the developmental group's facilitator. The *animateur* has a facilitative role but also a creative and energising role. The *animateur* motivates, stimulates, quite literally *animates* the group. This is perhaps similar to Boal's description of the 'joker'. Boal's translator and editor, Adrian Jackson, writes: 'The joker figure is, in various different contexts and combinations, the director, referee, facilitator and workshop leader' (1992, pxxiv). This is a difficult balancing act. However, the facilitator (or whatever she chooses to call herself) is always a member-participant of the group and always enables the group to become interdependent. As we have argued, this is a process and the facilitator must at times (particularly in the early stages of the group's development) help the group by directing, intervening and providing structure. The facilitator will always be working towards a greater degree of sharing with the participants on an equal, democratic basis, carefully questioning whether it is better to let the group search and find its own way even if this creates a measure of discomfort. The facilitator is able to distinguish between feeling safe and feeling uncomfortable. Sometimes, the greatest learning opportunities are created out of feelings of discomfort.

Feeding back   Feedback, or the response of participants to each other, is one of the most important operational concepts in developmental group work. Feedback should be an honest, straightforward, helpful sharing of reactions to and observations about how one's behaviour is affecting others. Constructive feedback is particularly difficult to give and the facilitator will model feedback right from the first session, enabling and encouraging participants to feed back to each other. As the group becomes interdependent, the facilitator provides the feedback less and less, instead reflecting back to the group, by asking open, probing questions like: How do we feel about what X just said? How do we think X feels at the moment? Does anyone want to say anything to X right now?

Planning group work sessions
Considering the stage of development the group has reached   When activities for developmental group work sessions are planned, it is important to consider the group's stage of development, for example, an activity that relies for its success on the establishment of trust

among group members will not be appropriate for a newly formed group. 'Ice-breaker' type activities or activities involving getting to know each other would be far more appropriate. Equally, icebreakers will not be appropriate for a well-established group (although energisers may be). Activities should always match the group's stage of development.

While the facilitator may have some ideas about the longer term plans for the group, each developmental group work session can only be planned after the previous session. We have argued that the facilitator's role is to enable democratic decision making and inter-dependence. As the group develops, the facilitator provides less direction and includes the group in planning for the following session. Ideas for activities in the following session often emerge during a group work session.

We argued above that groups work through processes and will not start to *perform* until they have passed through the forming, storming and norming phases. Group processes cannot be rushed and the facilitator enables the group to work towards deeper, more complex tasks like friendship/ relationship work, emotional work, voice work or conflict work. Outcomes of developmental group work may take time and it is important that this is understood so that whole school or staff expectations of the effects of developmental group work are realistic.

Where to find activities   A number of publications provide ideas for group activities. We mostly used *Games for Actors and Non-actors* (Boal, 1992) and *Gamesters Handbook* (Brandes and Phillips, 1977). Other materials that deal with social and emotional development are: *A volcano in my tummy* (Whitehouse and Pudney, 1996); *Anger in the classroom* (Leseho and Howard-Rose, 1994) and *Draw on your emotions* (Sunderland, 1993).

Forming the group: an example of planning the first session
Forming the circle: the facilitator asks the group to arrange the chairs in a perfect circle. If this is not achieved the first time, the facilitator asks what is wrong with the circle and how the group can put this right to create the perfect circle. It does not matter how many times the facilitator has to ask the group to put the circle right. For some

groups, this may take the whole of the first session. When the circle is right and the participants are comfortable and can all see one another, the facilitator asks the group to reflect on the potential use of a circle (see above).

An icebreaker: the next activity may be an icebreaker or energiser. The exact nature of this activity will depend on how well the group know each other. A name game is often useful even when participants know each other quite well.

In circle time literature, *a round* describes an activity that enables everyone to contribute. To take an example: the facilitator asks the group to say what they expect from it or how they want to feel when they walk out the door at the end of the session. The facilitator is a participant and contributes to the round. The facilitator may also wish to ask the group to say one thing that they fear about group work. Reflection on this activity gives a good indication of what the group processes may be and the roles the facilitator may have to assume to keep the group safe during the dependence phase. During reflection, the facilitator may wish to discuss her role in the group explicitly and consult them about what they will need and what roles they would like her to perform so as to address their fears and keep them safe.

An activity usually follows the round. The activity will depend on the participants and on the focus of the developmental group work. It may be 'string connections' or 'Columbian hypnosis', or a double circle in which participants are asked to talk about themselves to a partner whose role is to listen (but not speak or feed back verbally) for thirty seconds. One participant acts as a timekeeper and shouts 'Stop!' at the end of thirty seconds. The partner then introduces the participant to the group. Roles are then swapped and the activity is carried out a second time. The facilitator asks the group to reflect on the activity: how did it feel to listen without being able to talk? How do you know that someone is really listening to you? How did the group feel about having to introduce their partners?

In order for the group to feel closure, it is important to formally *adjourn*. Good adjourning activities, like good icebreakers, energise the group and bring them back into the circle. Rhythm games are good 'adjourners': using voice, hands and feet all the participants set up a rhythm together. After a few minutes, this can be slowly changed until a new rhythm emerges and so on, for several minutes (Boal, 1992, p89).

Measuring outcomes

The Qualifications and Curriculum Authority has recently published guidance and a set of criteria for assessing emotional and behavioural development (QCA, 2001). The guidance is the result of a research project commissioned by the Qualifications and Curriculum Authority and undertaken by researchers from the University of Birmingham School of Education Assessment Research Unit. Drawing on a range of existing knowledge and understanding, the Birmingham research team developed a set of criteria in three separate categories: learning behaviour, conduct behaviour and emotional behaviour. This framework provides a useful starting point for a baseline understanding of a student's difficulties and could be used to inform referrals to the developmental group. However, it also provides a tool for measuring the effects of the developmental group for individual students over time.

Practitioner reflection – keeping a diary

We have proposed that each developmental group session be planned after the last group, as a long term session plan would prevent the group's process towards interdependence and democratic decision making. In order to plan effectively, the facilitator must have some way of reflecting on the group's processes.

We have included a diary extract written by a developmental group work facilitator. There were ten participants, including two facilitators, one of whom led, while the other was a participant observer. The diary extract describes a group in the fairly early stages of development. The two facilitators reflected on the group processes together, but kept their own diaries. This decision was taken as a way of securing quality control in an attempt to introduce some – albeit limited – form of objectivity into the observations. The facilitators compared diary extracts before they planned the next session.

The extract documents the group's breakthrough from dependence to interdependence and trust. This surprised the facilitator, who reflects on whether she was able to keep the group safe during this breakthrough.

Extract from a diary:

> The show and tell that the group requested last week really moved the group forward. M started off with a stone, a 'shrinker' and ceramic potpourri bird. She said that the stone reminded her that everyone is precious to someone (as the 'ugly' stone is precious to her). The 'shrinker' makes people who 'get too big' smaller. We talked about the need to have a magnifier as well to make people who feel small bigger. I brought my crystal stone that is rough on the outside and has beautiful crystals on the inside. This generated a discussion about what we see on the outside (people's behaviours that are sometimes difficult to like) and what is on the inside – a link between observable behaviours and emotions.
>
> L brought in broken necklace with a very sad story about the violent deaths of her father and brother. She told us that her mother got her and her sisters out of the house to a grandparent. When they came back, they found her father murdered and the broken bit of necklace under a pillow. L became very upset during this activity. F started to cry during L's story as she has recently lost her dad from cancer. Death and loss are a major issue in the group: C and A have both lost grandfathers who were very important to them and L lost a baby sister.
>
> N brought in a photo of her twin cousins who are ten years younger than her. She also encouraged A to speak – not to feel embarrassed as no-one will tease her and there are no boys around.
>
> This gave A the confidence to talk about her glass beads which broke during the accident in which she was run over. She also discussed her grandfather's death and the fact that she had inherited his glass beads. The beads therefore carry both sadness and fear (the accident) and also memory and loss (of her grandfather).
>
> T and S showed their paired necklaces: puzzle pieces that fit together. This is a metaphor for their friendship. This encouraged F and J to show to show their paired necklaces: 'best' and 'friend'. (There are often friendship fallouts in the group – should we plan a

121

session around the 'puzzle' of friendship and the way 'pieces' of friendship do not always fit together?)

At the end of the activity, we reflected on the feelings this activity had generated for us. We also reflected on how the experience of death (and feelings of bereavement, loss and pain) are common to many of us in the group. We identified the following themes: death and loss, friendship, love. We discussed using these themes next week in image theatre as a way to explore them further.

We also talked about the talking wand and how this made turn taking more explicit. This was generally considered to be a good thing, as everyone gets a chance to talk. We also reflected on the formation of the circle: I asked if there was anything that the girls noticed about the circle and M pointed out that friends are still sitting together. After this, C and L asked to re-organise the circle so that friends sat separately from each other and we did 'string connections' again. C and L proposed that we pass the string with a statement beginning 'I admire . . . ' this time. They felt that this would lift our feelings and make us feel good about ourselves.

The re-organisation worked much better but we reflected that we still tended to pass the compliments to friends or within friendship groups. We wondered how we could extend friendship networks. C suggested that we might do 'guardian angels' for next week as this may extend friendship networks.

N has a repertoire of riddles (taught to her by her grandfather) and she asked the group if she could end with a riddle. M joined in and told her own riddle.

Holding the level of emotions expressed in the group was difficult. I'm not sure that I kept them safe enough. Partly, I didn't expect trust to emerge so quickly and felt unprepared. Although we have done work around confidentiality, I'm not sure that this ground-work is sufficient to hold the personal disclosures that were made. On the other hand, the show and tell activity seemed to generate a very powerful catharsis and the girls appeared to leave the group in good spirits. Group members were really working together and caring for each other. The group is norming more quickly than I anticipated. The girls are also leading on activities more quickly than I expected.

Developmental group work as action research

We have noted that the theoretical and operational origins of developmental work can be found in the action research and group dynamic theories of Kurt Lewin in the mid 20th century. In Lewin's action research model, the focus of the group is the use of group dynamics to influence the process of social change and to discover more effective ways of functioning as agents of social change. Cycles of planning, acting, observing and reflecting form the basic methodology of action researchers. Thus the smaller developmental group processes model the larger research methods. This is significant if participant 'spect-actors' are to engage in processes of social change. In a section exploring doubts and certainties, at the end of *Games for Actors and Non-actors*, Boal writes:

> Let us hope that one day – please, not so far in the future – we'll be able to convince . . . our government, our leaders, to do the same: to ask their audiences – *us* – what they should do, so as to make this world a better place to live and be happy in – yes, it is possible – rather than just a vast market in which we sell our goods and our souls.
>
> Let's hope.
>
> Let's work for it! (1992, p247)

Participatory action research through developmental group work is a way of asking our pupils what we should do to make schools better places to learn and be happy in. Let's work for it!

References

Aitken, J. (2001) Echoes down the centuries. *The Times Educational Supplement* 04/05/2001

Atweh, B., Kemmis, S. and Weeks, P. (1998) *Action Research in Practice: partnerships for social justice in education.* London: Routledge

Barnes, B., Ernst, S. and Hyde, K. (1999) *An Introduction to Groupwork.* London: Macmillan

Bayley, J. and Haddock, L. (1999) *Training Teachers in Behaviour Management.* London: SENJIT

Boal, A. (1992) *Games for Actors and Non-actors.* London: Routledge

Boal, A. (1998) *Legislative Theatre: using performance to make politics.* London: Routledge

Bradford, S. (2000) Disciplining practices: new ways of making youth workers accountable. *International Journal of Adolescence and Youth,* 9, pp45–63

Brandes, D. and Phillips, H. (1977) *Gamester's Handbook: 140 games for teachers and group leaders.* Cheltenham: Stanley Thorpe

Brown, M. and Gilligan, C. (1992) *Meeting at the Crossroads: women's psychology and girls development.* Cambridge MA: Harvard University Press

Centre for Studies in Inclusive Education (2000) *Index for Inclusion: developing learning and participation in schools.* Bristol: CSIE

Contratto, S. (1994) A too hasty marriage: Gilligan's developmental theory and its application to feminist critical practice. *Feminism and Psychology,* 4(3), pp367–77

Curry, M. and Bromfield, C. (1994) *Personal and Social Education for Primary Schools through Circle Time.* London: NASEN

Dean, C. (2000) Barber's online debut. *The Times Educational Supplement* 15/09/2000

DES (1978) *Special Educational Needs* (The Warnock Report) London: HMSO

DES (1989) *Discipline in Schools* (The Elton Report). London: HMSO

DfEE (2000) *Developing a Global Dimension in the School Curriculum* (Circular 09/00). London: DfEE publications

DfEE (1999) *Social Inclusion: pupil support* (Circular 10/99). London: The Stationery Office

DfEE (1994) *The Education of Children with Emotional and Behavioural Difficulties* (Circular 9/94). London: The Stationery Office

DfES (2001) *Special Educational Needs Code of Practice.* London, The Stationery Office

Gardner, H (1993) *Multiple intelligences: the theory in practice.* New York: Basic Books

Goleman, D. (1996) *Emotional Intelligence: why it matters more than IQ.* London: Bloomsbury

Henry, J. (2001) Help for the boys helps the girls. *The Times Educational Supplement* 01/06/2001

Hey, V. (1997) *The Company She Keeps: an ethnography of girls' friendships.* Buckingham: The Open University Press

Hey, V., Leonard, D., Daniels, H. and Smith, M. (1998) Boys' underachievement, special needs practices and questions of equity. *Failing Boys.* Epstein, D., Elwood, J., Hey, V. and Maw, J. (eds). London: Open University Press

hooks, b. (1994) *Teaching to Transgress: education as the practice of freedom.* New York: Routledge

Johnson, M. and Hallgarten, J. (2002) *From Victims of Change to Agents of Change: the future of the teaching profession.* London: Institute of Public Policy Research

Klein, R. (2001) Emotional literacy interest groups. *The Times Educational Supplement* 06/04/01

Leseho, J. and Howard-Rose, D. (1994) *Anger in the Classroom: a practical guide for teachers.* Canada: Detselig Enterprises

Long, R. (1999) *Friendships.* London: NASEN

Marshall, W. (1996) Professionals, children and power. *Exclusion from School: inter-professional issues for policy and practice.* Blyth, E. and Milner J. (eds). London: Routledge

Myhill, D. (2002) Bad boys and good girls? *Patterns of Interaction and Response in Whole Class Teaching. British Educational Research Journal,* 28(3) June

OFSTED (2000) *Evaluating Educational Inclusion: guidance for inspectors and schools.* London: The Stationery Office

Orbach, S. (1999) *Towards Emotional Literacy.* London: Virago

Ozga, J. (2000) Education: new Labour, new teachers. *New Managerialism, New Welfare.* Clarke, J., Gewirtz, S. and McLaughlin, E. (eds). London: Sage

QCA (1999) *The National Curriculum: handbook for primary teachers in England.* London: HMSO

QCA (1999) *The National Curriculum: handbook for secondary teachers in England.* London: HMSO

QCA (2001) *Supporting School Improvement: emotional and behavioural development.* London: QCA Publications

Robinson, J. (2000) An Introduction to Developmental Group Work. London: unpublished training materials

Robinson, K., Chairperson (2001) *All Our Futures: creativity, culture and education.* National Advisory Committee on Creative and Cultural Education. London: The Stationery Office

Rudduck, J. and Gray, J. http://www.standards.dfee.gov.uk/genderandachievement/data_1.2.1.html

References

Rudduck, J. and Flutter, J. (2002) Consulting young people in schools. http://www.consultingpupils.co.uk/

SEU (1999) *Teenage Pregnancy: report by the Social Exclusion Unit.* London: The Stationery Office

Shaffer, J. and Galinsky, D. (1974) *Models of Group Therapy and Sensitivity Training.* New Jersey: Prentice-Hall

Slater, J. (2000) Girls face career handicap. *The Times Educational Supplement* (Society section) 08/09/2000

Spivak, G. (1988) Can the subaltern speak? *Marxism and the Interpretation of Culture.* Nelson, C. and Grossberg, L. (eds). Urbana: University of Illinois Press

Sunderland, M. (1993) *Draw on Your Emotions.* Oxford: Winslow Press

Thomas, G., Walker, D. and Webb, J. (1998) *The Making of the Inclusive School.* London, Routledge

Tuckman, B. (1965) Developmental sequences in small groups. *Psychological Bulletin*, 63, pp384–99

Whitehead, J. Creating living educational theory from questions of the kind 'How do I improve my practice?' *Cambridge Journal of Education,* 19(1), pp41–52

Whitehouse, E. and Pudney, W. (1996) *A Volcano in my Tummy.* Gabriola Island: New Society Publishers

Appendix

Cross-curricular links to the National Curriculum

The table below explicitly links the aims of developmental group work to the key area of spiritual, moral, social and cultural development; and the key skill working with others. It explores cross-curricular links to the English, PSHE and citizenship curricula.

Knowledge, skills and understanding	Learning objectives

Group discussion and interaction (EN1 speaking and listening KS3 & 4)	1. To speak fluently and appropriately in different contexts
	   a. structure their talk clearly, using markers so that their isteners can follow the line of thought
	   g. evaluate the effectiveness of their speech and consider how to adapt it to a range of situations
	2. To listen, understand and respond critically to others, pupils should be taught to:
	   b identify the major elements of what is being said both implicitly and explicitly;
	   f. ask questions and give relevant and helpful comments.
	3. To participate effectively as members of different groups, pupils should be taught to:
	   b. take different views into account and modify their own views in the light of what others say;
	   d. take different roles in the organisation, planning and sustaining of groups;
	   e. help the group to complete its tasks by varying contributions appropriately, clarifying and synthesising others' ideas, taking them forward and building on them to reach conclusions, negotiating consensus or agreeing to differ.

Developing confidence and responsibility and making the most of their abilities (PSHE KS3)	1. Pupils should be taught to:
	   b respect the differences between people as they develop their own sense of identity;
	   d. to recognise the stages of emotions associated with loss and change caused by death, divorce, separation and new family members, and how to deal positively with the strength of their feelings in different situations.

Developing confidence and responsibility and making the most of their abilities (PSHE KS4)	Pupils should be taught: a. to be aware of and assess their personal qualities, skills, achievements and potential so that they can set personal goals; b to have a sense of their own identity and present themselves confidently in a range of situations; c. to be aware of how others see them, manage praise and criticism, and success and failure in a positive way and learn from the experience; d. to recognise influences, pressures and sources of help and respond to them appropriately.
Developing good relationships and respecting the differences between people (PSHE KS3)	3. Pupils should be taught: a. about the effects of all types of stereotyping, prejudice, bullying, racism and discrimination and how to challenge them assertively; c. about the nature of friendships and how to make and keep friends; e. the changing nature of, and pressure on, relationships with friends and family, and when and how to seek help; i. to negotiate within relationships, recognising that actions have consequences and when and how to make compromises; j. ...to recognise when others need help and how to support them.
Developing good relationships and respecting the differences between people (PSHE KS4)	Pupils should be taught: d. to work co-operatively with a range of people who are different from themselves; f. to deal with changing relationships in a positive way, showing goodwill to others and using strategies to resolve disagreements peacefully.
Developing a healthier, safer lifestyle (PSHE KS3)	2. Pupils should be taught: a. to recognise the physical and emotional changes that take place at puberty and how to manage these changes in a positive way.
PSHE KS3 – breadth of study	4. During the Key Stage, pupils should be taught the knowledge, skills and understanding through opportunities to: f. develop relationships [for example by working together in a range of groups and social settings with their peers and others;] g. consider social and moral dilemmas; i. prepare for change [for example by anticipating problems caused by changing family relationships and friendships].

PSHE KS4 – Breadth of study	4. During the Key Stage, pupils should be taught the knowledge, skills and understanding through opportunities to: f. develop relationships [for example, by discussing relationships in . . . groups].
Knowledge and understanding about becoming informed citizens (citizenship curriculum)	Pupils should be taught about: g. the importance of resolving conflict fairly.

Developing skills of participation and responsible action (citizenship curriculum)	3. Pupils should be taught to:
	  a. Use their imagination to consider other people's experiences and be able to think about, express and explain views that are not their own;
	  c. reflect on the process of participating.

Index